D0328937

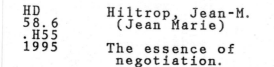

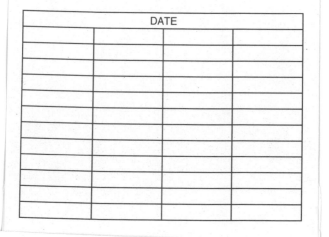

DATE			

BAKER & TAYLOR

The Essence of Negotiation

The Essence of Management Series

Published titles

The Essence of Total Quality Management
The Essence of Strategic Management
The Essence of International Money
The Essence of Management Accounting
The Essence of Financial Accounting
The Essence of Marketing Research
The Essence of Information Systems
The Essence of Personal Microcomputing
The Essence of Successful Staff Selection
The Essence of Effective Communication
The Essence of Statistics for Business
The Essence of Business Taxation
The Essence of the Economy
The Essence of Mathematics for Business
The Essence of Organizational Behaviour
The Essence of Small Business
The Essence of Business Economics
The Essence of Operations Management
The Essence of Services Marketing
The Essence of International Business
The Essence of Marketing
The Essence of Managing People
The Essence of Change
The Essence of International Marketing
The Essence of Personnel Management and Industrial Relations
The Essence of Competitive Strategy
The Essence of Business Process Re-engineering

Forthcoming titles

The Essence of Public Relations
The Essence of Financial Management
The Essence of Business Law
The Essence of Women in Management
The Essence of Mergers and Acquisitions
The Essence of Influencing Skills
The Essence of Services Management
The Essence of Industrial Marketing
The Essence of Venture Capital and New Ventures

The Essence of Negotiation

Jean M. Hiltrop
and
Sheila Udall

Prentice Hall

London New York Toronto Sydney Tokyo Singapore
Madrid Mexico City Munich

First published 1995 by
Prentice Hall International (UK) Ltd
Campus 400, Maylands Avenue
Hemel Hempstead
Hertfordshire, HP2 7EZ
A division of
Simon & Schuster International Group

Typeset in 10/12pt Palatino by
Keyset Composition, Colchester

Printed and bound in Great Britain by
Hartnolls Ltd, Bodmin, Cornwall

Library of Congress Cataloging-in-Publication Data

Available from the publisher

British Library Cataloguing in Publication Data

A catalogue record for this book is available from
the British Library
ISBN 0-13-349895-6

---

1 2 3 4 5   99 98 97 96 95

Contents

Acknowledgements

Our colleagues, friends, students and course members have shared their experiences and observations on negotiating practices throughout the years. We are deeply grateful to them for their ideas.

About the authors

JEAN M. HILTROP is currently Professor of Human Resource Management at the International Institute for Management Development (IMD) in Switzerland. He received his PhD in Psychology from Tufts University in the US and an MBA from the Management Centre of the University of Bradford in England. He has been involved in executive education for many years and has been appointed as a Professor and Director of the MBA programme at the Department of Applied Economic Sciences of the Katholieke Universiteit Leuven in Belgium. He has published numerous articles on labour mediation and the resolution of international conflicts, and has worked for many years as a negotiator in Europe, Asia and the United States. He is currently leading an international research project, which examines the impact of national culture on the negotiation practices and effectiveness of European companies.

SHEILA UDALL is an independent training consultant with 20 years experience in management training and development in both the public and private sectors. Starting her career as a training advisor in the engineering industry, she has also taught postgraduates in higher education and worked for a major local authority before becoming an independent consultant in 1989. She has helped to develop strategies and undertaken management development in many organizations such as ICI, Rolls Royce, British Aerospace, Cadbury Schweppes and Unilever. After taking an MA in Organizational Psychology she moved into management development in the public sector and now much of her work is focused on the issues involved in changing the culture of organizations, helping people with professional backgrounds to develop a more managerial orientation and the appropriate skills, including negotiating. She has co-authored a book called *People and Communication* and is researching another on the transition into management.

Introduction

Let us never negotiate out of fear. But let us never fear to
negotiate. (J.F. Kennedy, 1961)

Negotiation is such a common activity that most people probably do
it at some point every day, to sort out differences with other people,
or to get what they want. For managers, negotiation is not only
common but also essential for dealing with many organizational
problems. Whether working out next year's budget, setting the
delivery time of a product, building support for a new computer
system, or deciding the due date of a work assignment, people tend
to disagree and managers have to find a solution that is acceptable
to those whose co-operation is vital, including customers, suppliers,
peers, unions, bankers, government officials and a wide range of
other people.

Unfortunately, many managers do not think that negotiating will
solve problems so they do not handle situations as effectively as
they might. In fact, even after recognizing the need to negotiate,
many people still find the idea of negotiating with others uncomfort-
able, even distasteful; and, as a result, they prefer to resort to some
obvious, but often ineffective, techniques for dealing with difficult
situations, such as coercion, giving in, avoiding, blaming, fighting,
manipulating, referring the matter to a superior and so on.

Why are people afraid of negotiating?

This question can be answered by listening to the types of (self-defeating) comments which inexperienced managers make before embarking on negotiation. Two such comments are very common:

(1)   'I may lose something important.'
While this is an understandable and realistic concern, it is possible to take into account what both parties want, and develop win–win solutions. Negotiation does not have to be an unpleasant activity in which an agreement has to be reached at any cost. Goals are not necessarily mutually exclusive. In fact, many negotiators make themselves vulnerable because they have preconceived ideas. They may prepare, enter and conduct negotiations with not only an established view of what the issues are, but also with a view that the two parties' perception of the issues are directly opposed, that 'their win is our loss'. So they lock themselves into a strategy beforehand, with no option for responding to the obstacles, pitfalls and opportunities that are virtually certain to occur during the negotiation.

(2)   'I am not the right sort of person for this.'
Many people believe successful negotiating requires skills and abilities they do not possess, or do not want to be seen as possessing. They believe that people get what they want in negotiations through being tough, aggressive, dishonest, forceful and so on. While such tactics are sometimes used and can be effective if used appropriately, their importance is often greatly exaggerated. In fact there are other, more subtle tactics and strategies that can be used and will increase the likelihood of success in negotiation. Whilst there are people who get what they want through being dishonest, misleading and so on, this does not mean that these behaviours make successful negotiators. On the contrary, studies have shown that successful negotiators are often understanding and conciliatory. They are quiet and listen to the other side, explain their point of view without bullying, often concede when the other side has a valid point and even change their positions and preferred solutions. This suggests that to be successful, many people need to have a somewhat different view of what negotiation involves and what skills are needed to be effective.

What is the aim of this book?

In this book we aim to help you, as a manager, to become a better negotiator. Although some people are better natural negotiators than others, developing basic negotiation skills is far less difficult than it appears. It involves three main elements:

1. Acquiring **knowledge** of the basic principles of negotiation, the common (and costly) negotiating mistakes, and how to avoid them.
2. Developing interactive **skills** and the ability to communicate effectively.
3. Developing the **ability to recognize the specific feelings, values and beliefs** that other people have about proper conduct in negotiation, and to adjust one's attitudes and behaviour to the issues and personalities involved in the particular case.

Obviously, we cannot guarantee that every person who reads this book will become a good negotiator. Nor do we guarantee that we have the key to every problem you may encounter at the bargaining table. But, for people who have the potential of developing the personal qualities of a good negotiator, we strongly believe mastery of the practical insights and guidelines provided in this book will vastly increase their chances of resolving differences and achieving satisfactory solutions through negotiation.

How the book is organized

The book puts together a wide range of ideas and materials from a variety of sources. It is organized in six chapters:

Chapter 1. Describes various **basic principles of negotiation**, different aspects of the process and the common mistakes people make.

Chapter 2. Reviews the **key steps to effective negotiation**, including how to prepare your negotiations, how to open the discussions and how to make concessions.

Chapter 3. Is concerned with **within-group negotiation**, summarizing some of the factors contributing to success and some of the traps you can encounter when negotiating within groups, functions or departments.

Chapter 4. Looks at **inter-group negotiations**, such as pay bargaining between union and management, or the settlement of a commercial contract between customers and suppliers.

Chapter 5. Discusses how to manage **inter-cultural negotiations**. Clearly, negotiating becomes more difficult when the parties involved have different national and cultural backgrounds, and therefore do not share the same ways of thinking, feeling, and behaving. This section looks at some of these differences and their implications for negotiating.

Chapter 6. Is a **toolbox** or **a collection of instruments** that can be used to get a better understanding of the basic aspects of negotiating. Most of these instruments are in the form of check-lists. Once you know when and how to use these tools, the materials provided in the final part of the book will provide a practical aid for preparing your negotiation and determining which strategy to adopt at the bargaining table.

The Appendix contains a set of figures that can be used as presentation materials to summarize or illustrate the key learning points.

How to use the book

In our experience busy managers rarely have the time to sit down and read a book from cover to cover, so we have tried to make each chapter largely self-contained so that you should be able to dip into the book on a selective basis. Equally, we know that managers are usually looking for practical help (key learning points), before they explore ideas and information in more detail.

To help you get to grips with our main messages most efficiently we suggest that you:

• Read the **boxed sections** of each chapter first which summarize the essential learning points, the dos and don'ts, as well as potential pitfalls to avoid.

• Then read the **main text**, which illustrates and amplifies these points, drawing out their implications for negotiating.

- Finally, go through the **review questions and case studies** provided at the end of each chapter. This will improve your understanding of your personal negotiating abilities and help you practice the various skills needed to carry out actual negotiations.

Good luck!

1

Key Principles and Mistakes

In recent years there has been an explosion of management books, many seeking to assure you that if you do this, or say that, you will be successful in negotiation. Although the guidelines provided in these books often provide valuable clues to improving your performance in negotiating, we think it is important to be wary of neat packages or formulas supposedly guaranteeing success in every dispute. There are too many variables which affect the way people perceive and respond to each other, to predict precisely what to do in particular situations. Achieving a settlement through negotiation is not just a matter of applying a repertory of tactics and techniques in whatever conflict you are involved. In virtually all negotiations, you must adapt your strategy and behaviours to fit the needs of the particular case.

Negotiating is rather like taking a journey – you cannot predict the outcome until you have undertaken it. You may have planned a route only to find that the best way to get from here to there is not the planned one. Road works, traffic jams, fatigue, bored and fractious children may mean that you need to stop for a rest or take a detour. Similarly, with negotiating you need to prepare your strategy and tactics before entering a discussion, but there are no guarantees. You may even find that the planned approach is full of pitfalls and an alternative approach is needed in order to reach constructive agreement.

On the other hand, there are a number of basic principles or 'unwritten rules' which are common to all forms of negotiation and which you need to understand and pay attention to if you are to avoid costly mistakes.

In this chapter, we take a closer look at these basic principles and mistakes.

Basic principles

If you are going to play the game properly you'd better know the rules. (Barbara Jordan, US Congress, 1975)

What are these rules/principles?

In all but the least formal negotiations, it is important to keep in mind that:

1. Negotiating is a voluntary activity in the sense that either party can break away from or refuse to enter into discussion at any time.

2. A negotiation usually starts because at least one of the parties wants to change the *status quo* and believes that a mutually satisfactory agreement is possible.

3. Entering negotiations implies acceptance by both parties that agreement between them is required (or is desirable) before a decision will be implemented. If the matter can be decided unilaterally by one of the parties, there may be no point in committing oneself to the negotiating process.

4. Timing is a critical factor in negotiation. It plays an important role in influencing the overall climate and directly affects the ultimate outcome of the discussions.

5. A successful outcome in negotiation is not always winning at any cost or even 'winning', but getting what both sides want.

6. The progress of all types of negotiation, even when it is conducted through third parties, is strongly influenced by the personal values, skills, perceptions, attitudes and emotions of the people at the bargaining table.

What are the implications of these principles for an actual negotiation?

Putting all these principles together, a number of conclusions can be drawn which provide a starting point for gaining a better understanding and vision of what negotiation involves. We have to recognize several things:

(1) Negotiation does not have to be a verbal tug of war to be successful
In fact, if it is a tug of war, it is unlikely to be successful. The observation that negotiation usually starts because 'at least one of the parties believes that a mutually satisfactory agreement is possible' (Principle 2) means that negotiators are usually able to deal with each other without a fight, let alone the use of 'heavy' tactics leading to the escalation of conflict. In fact, most encounters between negotiators do not result in overt conflict. On the other hand, when overt conflicts do arise, if the parties employ offensive tactics that take them along the 'winding pathway' of dispute escalation, powerful and destructive forces are often unleashed. Needless to say, this is not the way to succeed in the long term.

(2) Successful negotiation involves the ability to (a) determine through observation and analysis the best means of persuasion and (b) put that persuasive approach into practice at the appropriate time
Negotiation is about influence and persuasion, not coercion and defeat. This means that the idea that, to be successful at negotiation, one needs to be forceful, hard-nosed, even capable of misleading others, is often greatly exaggerated. Negotiators who adopt this attitude are in reality likely to be ineffective. Because their attention is overwhelmingly focused on appearing strong, they are apt to miss opportunities for both sides to advance their priorities and self-interests through problem solving and a win–win settlement. Inevitably the other side will feel itself forced into a defensive and hostile position, instead of being enlisted as an ally in pursuit of mutually satisfactory agreement.

(3) Not all situations warrant 'negotiating treatment'
For example, it may not be possible or desirable to enter negotiations when:

- You are not in a position to bargain.
- You have the power or authority to impose your views.
- You do not have time to prepare effectively.
- Negotiating may damage your long-term objectives.
- You are too weak or inexperienced to deal with the other party.
- You are facing what you know is an unanswerable demand.

(4)   Because timing is important in negotiation, you need to recognize where you are in the negotiating process, and plan your actions (journey) accordingly

For instance, concessions if they are made in the opening phase will usually be premature and may get in the way of reaching a satisfactory (win–win) solution. You must plan for each move in the negotiation process. If you do not have time to plan, don't negotiate!

Common negotiating mistakes

A skilful negotiator will most carefully distinguish between the little and the great objects of his business, and will be as frank and open in the former, as he will be secret and pertinacious in the latter. (P. Stanhope, 1694–1773)
Believe one who has tried it. (Virgil, 80–19 BC)

Being human, most negotiators, even experienced ones, make mistakes. And once mistakes are made, it is difficult to make progress towards an agreement. As one observer remarked 'It is like spilling a glass of water on an absorbent surface. You can sop up the water and try to put it back in the glass, but you never get it all'.

What are the most common mistakes?

Based on his personal experience as a negotiator, John Illich (1992) suggests that managers are especially likely to make the following critical mistakes in negotiations:

1. Entering negotiations with a preset mental mindset.
2. Not knowing who has final negotiating authority.
3. Not knowing precisely what power they possess and how to use it effectively.
4. Entering a negotiation with only a general goal to be obtained upon the final outcome of the negotiation.
5. Failing to advance positions and arguments of substance.
6. Losing control over seemingly unimportant factors such as timing and the ordering of issues.
7. Failing to let the other side make the first offer.
8. Ignoring time and location as a negotiating weapon.

9. Giving up when negotiation seems to have reached a deadlock.

10. Not knowing the right time to close.

It is difficult to generalize about these mistakes. For example, with professional managers, time and location (Point 8) should make no big difference. Nevertheless, in our experience, *negotiations which 'go wrong' often do so for similar reasons*. We have called these reasons 'syndromes'.

Five such syndromes are described below. Each syndrome has symptoms which are the cluster of mistakes that negotiators typically make when failing to progress towards agreement for this particular reason. For each of the five syndromes, we suggest a number of 'remedies' that can be used to avoid or minimize the negative consequences of making the cluster of mistakes.

(1) The 'one-track' syndrome
This is where the negotiators have already decided what the facts of the case and the required solutions are, before the negotiating begins. They then enter the negotiation convinced that the other party will accept their solution. So they become 'a train running along one mental track, with no option for turning left or right to avoid the obstacles and pitfalls that are certain to occur along the way during every negotiation of consequence'.

Main symptoms:

- One of the negotiators begins the negotiation by stating that there are a number of key points to be covered and arranges them in an apparently logical order. These points are then worked through in a mechanical fashion, at relatively high speed, covering a lot of points, none in any great depth, regardless of the other party.

- Frequent interruptions to prevent the other party from talking at length on 'irrelevant' matters.

- Clear signs of frustration and/or non-acceptance on the part of the other party.

Underlying all of this may be a lack of faith on the part of one or both negotiators in their own skills, or a desire to cover too much ground in the time available, leading to trying to have everything cut and dried beforehand.

What are the potential remedies?

Clearly the best 'cure' to avoid making these mistakes is to be aware of their existence. Alternatively, a number of tactics and strategies can be suggested as 'antidotes' against the negative consequences of the one-track syndrome:

- View agendas as frameworks, which are useful as guides or check-lists, but which need not be rigidly adhered to at all times.
- Ask the other party to suggest items for the agenda and formulate a joint working plan for the discussions.
- Treat information as a hypothesis rather than a fact.
- Use interim summaries and restatements and reviews at the end of each topic or meeting to check understanding of points raised by the other party (for example, 'What we seem to have agreed so far is that . . .', or 'Would you agree that . . .?').
- Listen actively and look out for non-verbal cues of agreement, disagreement, surprise, frustration, etc., as well as the verbal content.

(2)   The 'win–lose' syndrome
The negotiators view, or come to view, the discussions as a contest or a debate which they are determined to win.

Main symptoms:

- Refusal to accept the validity of the other's views, claims and arguments.
- A large number of critical statements, personal attacks and emotional outbursts.
- A lot of closed questions and leading statements to gain compliance with preconceived ideas (for example, 'You must accept that . . .' or 'You do not seem able to understand that . . .').

The underlying cause of this approach may be based in a preconceived idea (backed by past experience) that negotiating is a battle rather than a problem-solving forum.

Remedies for dealing with the 'win–lose' syndrome:

- Ask more open questions to elicit the other party's views.

- Be prepared to listen to the other party.
- Avoid getting into defence–attack spirals.
- Resist the urge to reject or undermine every argument of the other party, even when you agree.
- Look for common ground.
- List points of agreement and disagreement.
- Ask yourself: What are my real interests in this dispute? How important is the long-term relationship with the other party? How can I make the other person concede without losing face?

(3) The 'random walk' syndrome
This is when the negotiation frequently jumps from one topic to another before coming to an agreed conclusion, or when the negotiators periodically return to the same topic without adding anything to the discussions.

Main symptoms:

- There is no summary of the issues agreed or discussed at the end of a meeting.
- When one of the negotiators attempts to summarize, the other party objects that s/he never agreed to these points.

The underlying cause of this syndrome is usually that the negotiators have not thought through the ramifications of the problem areas before the discussion, or are unwilling to face up to the conflicts that might arise if problem areas are probed too deeply.

Remedies for dealing with the 'random walk' syndrome:

- Think through likely problem areas before the discussion.
- Delay closure on a topic until a full agreed solution is arrived at.
- Use more probes to obtain detailed information about the problem area under discussion.
- Use more summarizing and paraphrasing to ensure that the other party understands your point of view.
- Be more tolerant of silence, allowing some thinking time or forcing the other party to talk.
- Spend more time on defining what the problem is.

- Have more adjournments to review the discussion and consider the way forward.
- Devote greater attention to agenda setting before the discussion of the issues begins.

(4)   The 'conflict avoidance' syndrome
In this situation, the parties do not talk about the issues underlying their conflict or are merely paying lip-service to them.

Main symptoms:

- No agenda setting.
- Asking open questions with no follow through.
- Rapid switches to more 'comfortable' topics.
- Unconditional concession making.
- Proposals are made as a 'gift'.

The underlying causes may be that one of the parties does not believe the problem is sufficiently serious to merit much attention and/or wishes to maintain an image of being a nice person. Another potential reason is that one of the negotiators wishes to have as painless an interaction as possible, and therefore identifies what the other party wants and gives it to him/her unconditionally.

Remedies for dealing with the 'conflict avoidance' syndrome:

- If the conflict is genuinely not serious, no remedial actions are needed.
- If the conflict is serious, attempt to influence the motivation of the parties (for example by identifying and prioritizing the issues).
- A recognition that giving in will not necessarily produce a good solution.
- Use of information gathering skills to identify and agree areas where agreement could be reached, and specific ways to achieve it.
- Where necessary, use of threats and promises to obtain commitment to achieving a joint solution.

(5)   The 'time capsule' syndrome
This is when the negotiators do not consider the circumstances or context in which the negotiation is taking place, either in terms of

the pressures on themselves or the other party, or the history of the relationship. They treat the situation in isolation and are surprised if the other person does not see the negotiation in the same light as themselves or introduces elements from past encounters especially if they were considered to be (lost) battles.

Main symptoms:

- One negotiator treats the encounter with a great deal more gravity than the other, and gets frustrated when the other party does not see things in a similarly serious light.
- One party is in a more highly charged emotional state.
- One party raises an issue that the other person thinks has nothing to do with the current dispute.

Underlying causes include the parties having different perceptions about the relationship and its current status due to insufficient reviewing of previous encounters, lack of thought about recent events, or lack of preparation for the current negotiation.

Key points for avoiding common mistakes

To avoid some of the most common and costly negotiation mistakes:

1. Do not interrupt the other party. Talk less and listen actively.
2. Ask open ended questions to build understanding.
3. Use paraphrasing, humour and positive comments.
4. Use adjournments to keep control over your team and discussions.
5. Set yourself a clear, specific and realistic goal before entering a meeting.
6. Summarize regularly.
7. List the points of explanation, interpretation and understanding.
8. Avoid weak language, such as 'We hope', 'We like', 'We prefer'.
9. Don't always criticize the other party. Look for common ground.
10. Avoid irritators. Value-loaded words like 'unfair' or 'unreasonable' tend to provoke a defensive or aggressive response.
11. Avoid diluting your own arguments by giving too many reasons for your proposal. It is better to have one or two good reasons for all your claims than to have ten weak reasons for each claim.
12. Avoid emotional outbursts, blaming, personal attacks or sarcasm.

Remedies for dealing with the 'time capsule' syndrome:

- At the beginning of each negotiation session, be clear about where the relationship stands.
- Consider the other party's priorities and pressures before and during the negotiation.
- Continuously check understanding of the other's point of view.
- Try to find solutions about which both parties can feel positive.

REVIEW QUESTIONS

Reviewing all the main points that have been made in this section:

1. How would you express your attitude to negotiating? If you enjoy it, say why. If not, why not?

2. What are the main characteristics of an effective negotiator? What improvement in your ability would you most like to achieve?

3. Without going into detail, think of ten different activities, which are in essence negotiations. What are the main situations in which you find yourself negotiating at work and at home?

4. Think of an example of situations where negotiating is inappropriate. How often have you been in this type of situation? Why was negotiating inappropriate?

5. Think of a recent negotiation that has happened at home or at work.
   - How efficiently was it handled on both sides? Was agreement reached, and if so how wise an agreement was it? Did relations improve, deteriorate or stay the same as a result?
   - What were the mistakes made by the parties in those negotiations – both the obvious and the less obvious? Why did these mistakes occur? How do they relate to the 'negotiation syndromes' identified in Chapter 1. Now that the conflict is resolved can you think of symptoms which at the time you did not notice?

6. Think of an occasion when you feel you were effective as a negotiator. What were you doing/not doing that made you feel effective?

7. Think of an occasion when you felt you were not effective as a negotiator. Can you now identify why you were not effective? Note down your thoughts and ideas on how you might have done things better.

2

Managing the Negotiation Process

Res nollunt diu mali administrari. (Things refuse to be
mismanaged for long.) (Marcus Aurelius, 121–180)

There are a number of ways to describe the various procedures
followed by negotiators; however, we believe that most negotiations
can be seen as a loosely ordered sequence of six distinct stages or
phases which can be presented in the following simple format:

1. **Preparation**: In which the negotiators identify the issues and
   range of objectives for each issue.
2. **Developing a strategy**: In which each party decides what
   strategy and style to adopt.
3. **Getting started**: In which each side presents their initial demand or case.
4. **Building understanding**: In which the negotiators justify their
   position and try to weigh up the other's position.
5. **Bargaining**: In which each party tries to get concessions.
6. **Closing**: In which final agreement is reached or the negotiations
   are terminated short of an agreement.

Some of these stages are more relevant to formal negotiations
between teams or organizations than to informal discussions between individual managers. However, even in a more informal
situation, the six steps provide a simple and practical framework for
managing your negotiations, and identify the skills and strategies
involved in this process. We recommend you use this six-step

approach in all your negotiations, as, whilst it is not a guarantee for success, it will help you to assess the situation accurately, select the best means of persuasion and implement your strategy effectively. It will also protect you from making some of the most common and costly mistakes mentioned earlier, and help you set objectives and time limits that work for, not against, you.

The six-step approach

1. Preparing for negotiation.
2. Developing your strategy.
3. Getting started.
4. Building understanding.
5. Bargaining.
6. Closing.

The following sections deal in some detail with the skills and activities associated with each stage of this approach (such as assessing relative strengths and weaknesses, setting the agenda, and getting and making concessions) and provide hints for improving your performance as a negotiator in each stage.

Step 1: Preparing for negotiation

Jewel in the crown of effective negotiation. Get this right and your performance in the negotiation dramatically improves. (G. Kennedy, 1993)

Good preparation is essential in negotiation. A poorly prepared negotiator demonstrates sooner or later that s/he does not know what s/he is talking about.

There are three basic elements in any preparation:

1. Setting bargaining objectives.
2. Assessing the other side's case.
3. Assessing relative strengths and weaknesses.

Let us consider each element in turn.

(1) Setting bargaining objectives

In negotiating like many other activities, it is vital to understand that 'if you don't know where you are going, you are liable to end up some place else'. What you need to do, therefore, is to think carefully and *prior to the actual negotiation* about what you are trying to achieve.

How to set objectives

When preparing, identify a range of objectives, rather than a single target point. This range includes:

1. A **top line** objective – the best achievable outcome.
2. A **bottom line** objective – the lowest, still acceptable, outcome.
3. A **target** objective – what you realistically expect to settle for.

Bargaining normally takes place between the top line objectives of the two negotiators, whereas agreement takes place between the parties' bottom line objectives. If the bottom line positions do not overlap, an agreement cannot normally be reached.

On the other hand, not all issues and disputes lend themselves to a range of objectives. For example, when some matter of principle is involved, the top and bottom lines may not really exist. Where this is the case, you should at least establish a realistic bargaining objective. It is crucial to have a clear goal in mind while negotiating.

While the most likely outcome of a negotiation is a compromise, this does not mean that the final agreement must be 'down the middle' of the negotiators' respective target objectives. In fact, better preparation, more skilful bargaining or more power usually means that one of the parties will finish closer to his/her target point.

How to define your bargaining range

A considerable amount of information is required to establish your objectives for the negotiation. Some of it will be available during your preparation, other information will have to be gathered during the early stage of the discussion.

As you decide your bargaining objectives, try not to get so wrapped up in contemplating what you can win that you forget to calculate what you can lose. Ask yourself 'What is the most I can lose in this negotiation?'. This is your *best alternative to no agreement* (commonly referred to by its acronym BATNA) and it will help you define and decide on your target objective in a realistic way. It also determines your degree of generosity and the level of your 'walk-away' position. If you have little to lose, your downside risk is small. You can afford to be generous. On the other hand, if you stand to lose a great deal, you must choose and use your objectives with great care.

In defining your BATNA, ask yourself:

- How far can I go? When should I stop negotiating?
- What will happen if I stop negotiating?
- Do I need the other party for implementing my solution?
- Do they need me?

Normally, the better your BATNA, the stronger your bargaining position, and the more demanding you can afford to be. However, to assess bargaining power, you also need to consider the other party's best alternative to non-agreement.

If possible, one of your bargaining objectives should be to help the other party to feel satisfied with the outcome.

Finally, in negotiation, firmness and clarity are a strength. Therefore, as a rule, your BATNA and bargaining objectives should not be altered unless the underlying assumptions change.

(2) Assessing the other side's case

To plan your negotiation, you may have to make assumptions about the other side's likely reactions to your demands. Assumptions are best guesses, and must be tested. If you act without testing your assumptions you may inadvertently spend a lot of energy in resisting something the other party is not demanding or demanding something the other is not resisting.

What are the key stages ?

As early as possible in your preparation and negotiation, you need to carry out the following activities:

1. Try to **establish** what the other party's **claims** are and what they are seeking to achieve.
2. **Probe** whether specific **problems** or concerns lie behind their questions or claims.
3. **Exchange** factual **data** in advance of negotiations.
4. **Consider** what **facts and arguments** the other party is likely to use in support of their claim.

5. Consider the possible existence of a hidden agenda. **Look for underlying issues** which may influence the conduct and outcome of the negotiations or cause delay and confusion during negotiation.

(3) Assessing relative strengths and weaknesses

Strength is the power or influence you can exercise over the actions of the other party.

What kinds of power are there?

Power and influence may take many forms, for example:

- Decision-making authority (you're the boss).
- Superior knowledge of the issues in dispute.
- Superior financial resources.
- More time to settle the case.
- The moral strength of the actual case.
- The determination or persistence of the negotiator.
- Better preparation.
- More experience in negotiating.

What should you bear in mind when assessing your strengths and weaknesses?

- Power is of no use unless both parties know about it and have a similar view of its extent.
- If you are stronger than the others but they do not know, then you have no effective power. If you are weak and they do not know, you are stronger than you think you are.
- If you are stronger and both parties know it, then your basic use of this advantage in the negotiation will be to remind them of the consequences of not conceding to your suggestions.
- The skilled negotiator uses or threatens to use his/her power to influence and persuade the other party rather than to defeat them.
- You may be the weaker of the two parties but you are never totally powerless.
- When your case is really hopeless, plan to minimize your losses rather than to defend the case.

- Experienced negotiators will think very carefully before they take full advantage of the other side's weaknesses. Recognizing the need to 'live together', however uncomfortably, gives each side some negotiating strength.

- Negotiating skill is no substitute for lack of negotiating strength. Skill can only offer short-lived advantages.

Your own negotiation position can sometimes be strengthened by identifying and tactfully reminding the other party of sanctions which are available if negotiations fail. These sanctions may be financial, legal or emotional, or may relate to the effect of a particular outcome on an organization's or on an individual's reputation, image or self-esteem. Displays of emotion may occasionally be beneficial provided that they are sincere and used consciously. However, try to avoid emotional outbursts.

Key points for preparing your negotiation

When preparing for negotiation, do the following things as often and thoroughly as possible:

1. Identify the real issues in dispute.
2. Ask yourself :
   - What are our basic underlying concerns?
   - What are our 'must get' objectives?
   - What are our 'like to get' objectives?
   - What are our 'intend to get' objectives?
   - What are the criteria by which we will judge whether the negotiation has been a success or a failure?
   - If we fail to achieve our objectives, do we re-negotiate?
3. Determine your walk-away position.
4. Examine what sources of power you possess.
5. Assess your relative strengths and weaknesses.
6. Determine your strategy for the first meeting.

If you are negotiating as a team, also consider the following:

7. Decide clearly who will be the spokesperson during the discussions.
8. Determine the roles of the other team members.

Step 2: Developing a strategy

Always choose the way that seems best, however rough it may be. Custom will render it easy and agreeable. (Pythagoras, c. 500 BC)

Planning your overall strategy is an important part of preparing to negotiate. Yet, at the same time it is important not to make over-elaborate strategic plans beforehand because if the negotiation takes a direction that you had not anticipated then you will need to adjourn to re-examine your approach.

Key points in developing your strategy

- What questions should we ask in the first session?
- What questions are they likely to ask?
- How will we answer these questions?
- What is our opening position?
- Do we have enough *factual* data and information to support this position?
- If not, what extra information could be available?

When you are negotiating as a team, also consider the following questions:

- Who will lead the discussion?
- Who will check understanding (verify facts)?
- Who will ask what questions?
- Who answers the other side's questions?
- Who will work to reduce tension and show concern for people?

In addition to determining your strategy, there are two questions to be answered before entering the negotiation:

(1) What style will I adopt?

Although you may not often think of it this way, everyone has his or her own characteristic approach, or style, when it comes to managing conflict. For example, a particular person may be characterized as being more (or less) aggressive, dominating, inflexible, dishonest, constructive, compliant, co-operative, competitive and so on. According to Thomas and Kilmann (1974), these different approaches can be grouped into five distinct categories as follows.

(1) Collaborating

The collaborator's approach to conflict is to manage it by maintaining interpersonal relationships *and* ensuring that both parties to the conflict achieve their personal goals. This attitude towards conflict is one in which the individual acts not only on behalf of his or her self-interest but on behalf of the opposing party's interests as well. Recognizing that a conflict exists, the collaborator utilizes appropriate conflict management methods to manage the situation. This is a co-operative approach which requires both parties to take a 'win–win' stance – it also requires time, energy and creativity.

(2) Compromising

This approach assumes that a win–win solution is not possible. The compromiser adopts a negotiating stance which involves a little bit of winning and a little bit of losing, both with respect to the goals and the relationships of the parties involved. Persuasion and manipulation dominate this style. The objective is to find some expedient, mutually acceptable solution which partially satisfies both parties. The compromise posture means that both parties adopt a 'mini-win–mini-lose' stance.

(3) Accommodating

The accommodator's approach to conflict involves maintaining the interpersonal relationship at all cost, with little or no concern for the personal goals of the parties involved. Giving in, appeasing and avoiding conflict are viewed as ways of protecting the relationship. This is a yield or 'lose–win' posture, in which the accommodator's stance towards managing the conflict is to yield–lose, allowing the other party to win.

(4) Controlling

The controller's approach to conflict is to take the necessary steps to ensure that his or her personal goals are met, whatever the cost to the relationship. Conflict is viewed as a win or lose proposition, with winning somehow equated with status and competence. This is a power-oriented approach in which you use whatever power seems appropriate to defend a position which you believe is correct or simply attempt to win.

(5) Avoiding

The avoider views conflict as something to be shunned at all costs. A central theme of this style is evasiveness, which results in a high degree of frustration for all parties involved. Personal goals are usually not met, nor is the interpersonal relationship maintained. This style might take the form of diplomatically diverting an issue, postponing an issue until a better time, or simply withdrawing from a threatening situation. It is a leave or lose–win posture, in which the avoider's stance is to leave–lose, allowing the other party to win.

What is your preferred style?

To assess your preferred approach to negotiating, complete the questionnaire below, and transfer your responses to the 35 statements to the appropriate space in the scoring table. The style with the highest total represents your most preferred negotiating style. If two or more styles have the same total, you probably use both styles and use them equally or alternatively. The style with the lowest score is your least preferred approach which may be difficult to adopt even when it is appropriate. The profile will be representative of your general philosophy towards negotiating, depending on the extent to which your responses were candid.

ASSESSING YOUR CONFLICT MANAGEMENT STYLE

This questionnaire is based on Kenneth Thomas and Ralph Kilmann's *Conflict Mode Instrument*. It enables you to gain insight into strategies you might choose to handle interpersonal conflicts, and to become more aware of your characteristic approach, or style, in managing conflict, particularly under stress.

The questionnaire contains 35 statements about the way in which people may choose to behave in conflict situations. Choose a single frame of reference (e.g. work-related conflicts, family conflicts, social conflicts) and keep that frame of reference in mind when responding to all the statements.

For each statement, indicate the extent to which you feel that statement is descriptive of you by using the following scale:

1 = You *strongly disagree* with this statement.
2 = You *disagree* with this statement.
3 = You *slightly disagree* with this statement.
4 = You *neither agree or disagree* with this statement.
5 = You *slightly agree* with this statement.
6 = You *agree* with this statement.
7 = You *strongly agree* with this statement.

There are no right or wrong responses. The survey will be helpful to you only to the extent that your responses accurately represent your characteristic behaviour or attitudes.

When facing conflicts with another person, I typically do the following things:

Rating

———— 1. I avoid the person.

———— 2. I change the subject to a neutral topic.

———— 3. I try to understand the other person's point of view.

———— 4. I try to turn the conflict into a joke.

———— 5. I listen to the other's feelings.

———— 6. I admit that I am wrong, even if I do not believe I am.

———— 7. I give in.

———— 8. I demand more than I would actually settle for.

———— 9. I use my power to prevent the other from reaching his or her goal.

————10. I try to find out specifically what we agree and disagree on.

————11. I try to reach a compromise.

————12. I pretend to agree.

————13. I move towards problem solving as best I can.

————14. I get another person to decide who is right.

————15. I suggest a way in which both I and the other gain something.

————16. I threaten the other party.

————17. I fight it out physically.

————18. I try to clarify what the other's goals are.

————19. I complain until I get my way.

————20. I give in, but let the other person know how much I am suffering.

————21. I apologize.

————22. I give up some points in exchange for others.

————23. I get the best deal I can no matter what.

————24. I postpone discussing the issues.

————25. I look for a middle ground.

————26. I avoid hurting the other's feelings.

————27. I get everything out in the open.

————28. I sacrifice my interests for the relationship.

————29. I split the difference between our positions.

————30. I give up some points in exchange for others.

————31. I let the other party take responsibility for finding a solution.

————32. I try to stress the points on which we agree.

————33. I try to get the other person to settle for a compromise.

————34. I try to convince the other person of the logic of my arguments.

————35. I try to meet the objectives of the other person.

Negotiating style scoring table

Collaborator:	Statement	Score
	3	————
	5	————
	10	————
	13	————
	18	————
	27	————
	32	————
	Total:	————

Compromiser:	Statement	Score
	11	————
	15	————
	22	————
	25	————
	29	————
	30	————
	33	————
	Total:	————

Accommodator:	Statement	Score
	6	————
	7	————
	20	————
	21	————
	26	————
	28	————
	35	————
	Total:	————

Controller:	Statement	Score
	8	————
	9	————
	16	————
	17	————
	19	————
	23	————
	34	————
	Total:	————

Avoider:	Statement	Score
	1	————
	2	————
	4	————
	12	————
	14	————
	24	————
	31	————
	Total:	————

Negotiating style profile

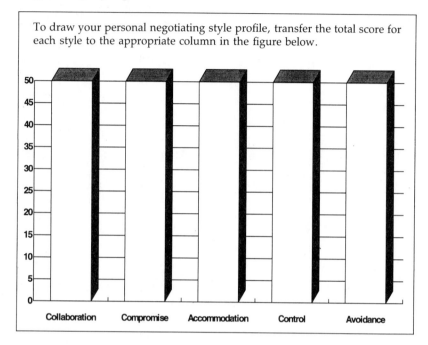

To draw your personal negotiating style profile, transfer the total score for each style to the appropriate column in the figure below.

How do you know which approach to choose?

Four basic points to remember about people's negotiating styles are that:

1. People develop their styles/approaches for reasons that make sense to them.

2. Although many people seem to prefer the collaborating style, it is important to understand that no single negotiating style is appropriate in all circumstances. No one style/approach is better than another in every situation. Sometimes people in different situations require different techniques – you may not be able to talk to your boss in the same way that you talk to your best friends.

3. People often change their styles/approaches in order to adapt to the demands of new situations. Most of us use different techniques for resolving conflicts with different people, but at the same time we often use a limited number of techniques.

4. Professional negotiators typically aim for a collaborating style but are prepared for confrontation. Keep in mind that they have

to continue to prove to those they represent that they are capable, successful and strong. Competitive behaviour, therefore, might be 'playing to the gallery' as much as attacking you or defending themselves.

Thus, as part of determining an overall strategy, you should be ready to change your style in either direction as the situation demands.

WHEN TO USE THE FIVE NEGOTIATING STYLES

Thomas (1977) identified the particular situations in which each style works best. He suggests that:

Controlling is best when:

- Quick, decisive action is vital (e.g. in emergencies).
- An important issue requires unpopular action.
- You know you are right.
- The other party would take advantage of co-operative behaviour.

Collaborating is best when:

- The issues are too important to be compromised.
- The objective is to integrate different points of view.
- You need commitment to make the solution work.
- You wish to build or maintain an important relationship.

Avoiding is best when:

- The issues are not important.
- There are more pressing issues to tackle.
- There is no chance of achieving your objectives.
- The potential 'aggravation' of negotiating outweighs the benefits.
- People need to cool down and regain their perspective.
- Others can resolve the conflict more effectively.
- You need time to collect more information.

Accommodating is best when:

- You find out that you are wrong.
- You wish to be seen as reasonable.

- The issues are more important to the other party.
- You wish to build 'credits' for later issues.
- You wish to minimize loss when you are in a weak position.
- Harmony and stability are more important.

Compromising is best when:

- Issues are important but you cannot afford to be too controlling.
- The relationship is important but you cannot afford to accommodate.
- Opponents of equal power are committed to mutually exclusive goals.
- You need to achieve temporary settlements to complex issues.
- You need to find an expedient solution under time pressure.
- It is the only alternative to no solution.

(2) What tactics will I use?

There are a number of additional aspects of the negotiation which need to be considered and require decisions to be made during the preparation. These include:

1. **Where to negotiate?** Most negotiators feel more confident on home ground, but for major, formal negotiations, the use of a neutral location may be desirable.

2. **When to negotiate?** Timing is a crucial factor in negotiation. Ensure sufficient time is allocated to allow adequate preparation and negotiation. In particular, avoid starting negotiations on the spur of the moment.

3. **How to start the first meeting?** Careful attention to how the first meeting is conducted is an important preparatory tactic. Consider the goals and objectives of the first meeting seriously, because they have the ability to shape the climate and outcome of the negotiation process.

The following list of tactics suggested by Atkinson (1975) may help you to decide what is most appropriate.

To obtain information:

The direct question	'What is it you are really looking for?'
Using sectorial interest	'I appreciate you cannot speak for all employees, but how does the sales department view this?'

Speaking to the silent	'You have been listening carefully to our discussions. 'So what do you think about . . .?'
The incomplete brief	'It would appear you have not been given the most recent figures. The latest report shows that . . .'
Blow hot–blow cold	'You can understand my colleague feels very upset about this and is ready to go to court. I wish we could avoid this confrontation. Can you tell me . . .'

To support your arguments and position:

Highlighting strengths	'Of course, you realize that we are obliged to talk to other potential suppliers.'
Minimizing weaknesses	'We would like to get this problem solved quickly, but we are not stuck for time.'
The precedent	'This solution has already been adopted by your competitors.'

To delay indicating your position:

The deferred response	'Yes I can give you these figures, but first tell me more about . . .'
Total avoidance	'This is an interesting question. However, I would like to know more about . . .. Can you tell me why?'

To undermine the arguments of the other party:

The credibility gap	'There appear to be some inconsistencies between what you and your colleague said earlier. Perhaps you can clarify . . .?'
Question the facts/source	'Your information says that . . .. However, our information is different. In fact, our sources tell us that . . ..'
Question the assumptions	'You say that . . .. Could you tell me on what this is based?'
Question the conclusions	'You have made this statement. Can you tell me how you came to this conclusion?'
Noting the omission	'I agree this is important, but you have not mentioned . . ..'
Amplifying the weakness	'These are interesting, but I am not convinced by your arguments. Take for instance . . . (the weakest argument).'

Suggesting a revision	'This data is three years old. We feel the present situation is somewhat different. Perhaps a revision is needed.'
Highlighting consequences	'Your conclusion is correct, but let's just have a look at what this could mean for your organization.'
Painting the picture	'Here is where you stand to gain from accepting our proposals.'

To generate movement:

Signal readiness to move	'I think we now have a pretty good idea of what is in each other's mind. Let's get down to the issue of . . .'
Make conditional offers	'If you change your offer on . . ., I am prepared to reconsider my demand for. . .'
Linking issues	'Do you think that it may be useful to look at issues A and B together?'
Suggest an adjournment	'You have heard my proposal. Perhaps we should adjourn to let you consider it and then come back with a revised offer.'
Appeal to norms	'Last time I agreed to help you out. Well it's your turn now, so give me a better offer on . . .'
Putting on pressure	'Let's get this settled and then we can move on to issues that are more important for the two of us.'
Come clean	'To be honest, I do not care much about this item. Now if you tell me what is really important to you, we can perhaps come to a win–win solution.'

To save face or reduce tension:

Use humour	A little boy asked J. F. Kennedy: 'Mr. President, how did you become a war hero?' Reply: 'It was involuntary. They sank my boat.'
The misunderstanding	'When you said . . ., I thought you were referring to . . . I would never have made this claim if I had known that . . .'
Changed circumstances	'We would like to change our claim as the circumstances surrounding this case have changed. Our new proposal is . . .'

Quid pro quo	'If we both revise our original positions slightly, we have an agreement. If you . . ., then I am willing to abandon my claim for . . .'
Special case	'Normally I could not agree with this, but in this special case, I am prepared exceptionally to . . .'
Use a third party	Involve a conciliator, or suggest their opinion be sought.

Step 3: Getting started

First learn the meaning of what you say, and only then speak. (Epictetus, c. 60 BC)

The very beginning is probably the most important part of any negotiation, because it will set the tone for all that follows.

There are two key elements for getting started:

1. Opening the negotiation.
2. Setting the agenda.

(1) Opening the negotiation

The progress of a negotiation is influenced significantly by the opening statement of the two parties, for a number of reasons:

1. It conveys **information** about a party's attitudes, aspirations, intentions and perceptions of the other party and the issues in dispute.

2. It has the ability to shape the **climate** of the negotiation. The typical period in forming this effect is short – very short: it takes usually a matter of seconds at the beginning of the negotiation, certainly not more than minutes. Within this very short period, from the parties coming together at the outset of negotiations, you have the opportunity to create either a positive and constructive atmosphere or a hostile, tough, distrustful and/or uncompromising atmosphere. Once created, the latter is likely to be very durable and almost impossible to improve subsequently.

3. It may be used by the parties to explore the other side's overall **posture** before deciding on their own.

4. It can be used by the parties to establish the **negotiation range**.

Who should speak first?

For the reasons noted above, it may be to your advantage to get the other party to make their opening statement first. This will avoid a serious miscalculation as their style may be significantly more co-operative or competitive than you expected.

One way of securing this opening position is to volunteer a brief rehearsal of the background before full negotiations begin. Then ask them to give an idea of their current position.

In most negotiations, the first position of either side has more effect on the final outcome than any of the later moves. The skill comes in setting yours at the right level and responding to theirs in the right way.

Where should you pitch your opening position?

The convention is that you always demand more than you expect to get and offer less than you expect to give. Therefore, your opening position should in general be pitched 'well away' from where you hope to settle. 'Well away' openings give you time and space to negotiate for your target settlement.

There also is plenty of evidence to show that the more you ask for, the more you get. However, the real gains from an extreme opening position must be weighed against the considerable loss of face that results from a big 'climb down' which may be necessary to avoid a breakdown in the negotiation.

How do you respond to the other's opening position?

If it is convention to ask for more than you want, then it must also be convention to reject first and other early offers. Thus, never accept a first offer, however attractive it may seem. If you ignore this opening convention and make your 'best offer first', the other party is unlikely to do the same. Instead, they will reject what you propose and use that as a starting place for their negotiation.

(2) Setting the agenda

To be effective, the negotiators need a common understanding of what is to be discussed and why. The subject, scope and purpose, therefore, need to be agreed before negotiations commence.

For formal negotiations, this definition of the agenda should be in

Key points for opening the negotiation

The opening moves in a negotiation are critical, as they:

- Convey information about your attitude and aspirations.
- Shape the negotiation climate.
- Make it clear who is the more experienced, confident, stronger and better informed party.

Therefore, when opening the negotiations, be prepared to:

1. Introduce yourself and your team partners.
2. Cover the 'process' issues first. Why are we meeting, for how long? Who is going to be involved? Who is going to talk first, about what matters? When will you or the other side respond?
3. Emphasize the importance of getting agreement together from the outset.
4. Give your general views on the issues to be covered. Especially mention your underlying concerns.
5. Obtain a briefing on the other side's view.
6. Keep the first meeting short and exploratory; do not enter into a discussion of the issues involved.
7. Adjourn after each side has expressed its views on the broad field to be covered. Summarize before you leave.
8. Agree what you and the other party will do when you resume the negotiations.
9. Listen for your opponent's use of non-absolute and qualified statements of his position, or references to his inhibitions.

---

writing, providing the other party with time to prepare arguments and responses. However, do not be bound by the assumed 'legitimacy' of a written agenda. The agenda always remains negotiable.

Step 4: Building understanding

Many things are lost for want of asking. (George Herbert, 1593–1633)

This phase of the negotiation has three components:

1. Getting information.
2. Testing arguments and positions.
3. Using timing and adjournments.

(1) Getting information

In negotiation, information is power. The more information you can get from the other side the better.

How to get information?

It seems obvious that to gain information, you should ask questions. However, in real negotiations it is remarkably easy to get so wrapped up in presenting your own case that you forget to ask questions at all.

The quality of the information provided by the other party depends largely on the type of questions asked. Anyone who has seen a skilful lawyer break down a carefully constructed lie knows the value of effective questions. To maximize the amount of information provided by the other person, you should ask the following types of questions:

- **Open questions** to obtain general information concerning some issue or topic. For example 'Tell me about . . .', 'Could you describe what you think are . . .', 'Could you tell us more about . . .?'.

- **Probing questions** to elicit more information about a particular issue or claim. For example 'Could you tell me more about . . .?, 'What do you mean by . . .?'.

- **Closed questions** for establishing specific points of fact and receiving simple yes and no responses. For example 'What is the exchange rate?', 'Did you receive our proposal?'

- **Hypothetical questions** to encourage the other party to explore his or her ideas or feelings about a particular subject. For example 'How much would your price change if we increased our order by 10%?'.

What else can you do to encourage the other side to disclose information?

In addition to asking questions, there are a number of other techniques which can be useful for getting the other side to tell you more about their case, such as:

- **Lubricators** such as 'Yes', 'Go on', 'mm', and 'Ah-ha' indicating to the other party that you are listening and want them to continue.

Five functions of questions in negotiation

1. **To draw or focus attention:** Give indicators of what you are going to say. For example: 'Can I ask you a question about your proposal?' or 'Can we talk about price now?'. This technique reduces uncertainty and prepares the other's mind for what is coming.

2. **To get more specific information:** Typically the words to introduce this type of question are: who, what, where, when and how.

3. **To give information:** Questions can also be used to signal agreement or potential movement. For example: 'Could you help me solve this problem?' or 'Is this the only option we have?'.

4. **To get the other party to move:** For example 'Can you come back with a revised offer in the next meeting?' or 'Is this your final offer?'.

5. **To bring the other party's thinking to a conclusion:** For example 'Can you summarize your proposals?' or 'How about having a brief adjournment?'.

- **Comparisons** to get the other party to explore facts in a new light or reveal his or her own needs, values and opinions. For example 'What are the relative merits of this proposal?'.

- **Silences** for signalling that enough has been said and for indicating indignation or non-acceptance of views where frustration or emotion is being expressed.

- **Bridges** to provide a smooth transition between one topic and the next. For example 'I think that is all we need to say on that topic, now let's turn to . . .'.

- **Repeating or paraphrasing** what the other party has just said to check the accuracy of understanding or to crystallize ideas which have not been clearly expressed. For example 'What you seem to be telling me is that . . .'.

- **Summaries** to draw together all the major points at the end of a meeting or at the end of a particular section of the discussion before proceeding to the next topic. It can also help in gaining commitment to action. For example: 'What we seem to have discussed and decided so far is . . .'.

(2) Testing arguments and positions

Having obtained more information from the other party, their case should be tested. In particular, when testing the other side's case, you should look for the following flaws or distortions in the arguments of the other negotiator:

- Factual errors or omissions.
- Faulty logic.
- Selective use of statistics.
- Hidden agendas.
- Misrepresentation of priorities.

In this phase of the negotiation it is extremely important that you allow the other side to make their case fully before you reply. This means that you:

- **Do not interrupt** the other party's responses to your questions.
- **End each statement with a direct question.**
- **Say only what is necessary.** Remember that professional negotiators spend a lot more time listening than talking.
- **Summarize regularly what has been said.** Be careful to use your own words rather than mimicking or parroting what has been said by the other party.
- **Avoid being side-tracked.** New issues may be introduced into the negotiation as a diversion, or to provide opportunities for trade-offs between parts of a bargaining package.

Above all, never give information unless you get something useful in return.

COMMON FLAWS IN THE USE OF INFORMATION

Research has shown that people consciously or unconsciously rely on mental shortcuts or assumptions to help to manage the storage and retrieval of information. These short-cuts serve people well most of the time, but in negotiating, they can distort information handling and decision making. The following short-cuts and assumptions are especially common and problematic in negotiation:

(1) The fixed-pie assumption
This leads to the conclusion, often prematurely and faulty, that the two parties' interests are directly opposed, that 'your win is my loss', and hence encourages contentious behaviour.

(2) Illusionary conflict

Sometimes disputes involve issues in which the parties believe there are opposing interests when none exist. In other words, the negotiators assume conflict where there is agreement, but fail to realize it and unwittingly try to extract concessions from the other negotiator.

(3) Reactive devaluation

Negotiators tend to devalue concessions offered by the other party, simply on the basis of knowledge that the other person has offered them.

(4) Negotiation scripts

Most people hold intuitive theories about the process of negotiation. Among other things, these theories include assumptions about the behaviour that is fair or appropriate to expect from the other party, as well as what needs to be done to extract concessions.

(5) Rigid thinking

Negotiation can easily promote rigid thinking, which involves a tendency to see things 'black or white'. Rigid thinking, in turn, inhibits creativity and effective problem solving.

(6) Over-confidence

People typically enter negotiations with the belief that the other party will make greater concessions than they will. This over-optimism can lead to carelessness and unconditional concession making.

(7) Over-simplification

This involves making decisions solely on the basis of the most obvious characteristics of the situation or other negotiator, and ignoring more subtle features that would permit a more balanced decision.

(8) Risk aversion

Most people are motivated to minimize loss more than they are motivated to maximize gain. Also, a loss is generally perceived as more negative than an equivalent gain is perceived as positive. This implies that it is harder to concede when a concession is 'framed' in terms of 'loss' than when it is framed as a 'failure to gain'.

(3) Using timing and adjournments

In planning and conducting negotiations, positive attention should be paid to the duration of bargaining sessions, formal presentations and individual contributions to the discussion. In our experience, one individual session should rarely exceed two hours, a formal presentation 15 to 20 minutes, and an informal contribution 2 to 3

minutes. Longer discussions often lead to boredom, loss of attention, fatigue and/or unproductive exchanges related to the 'random
walk' syndrome.

How to use adjournments?

Adjournments can be used as powerful aids to negotiation. You
should use them whenever you find yourself in a situation with the
following conditions.

1. You need a few moments to absorb and consider the impact of
   important new information that has an effect on your strategy or
   position.

2. You recognize an important change in climate or style on the
   part of the other party.

3. A strategy or a particular tactic being followed proves ineffective, and a new strategy or tactic needs to be developed.

4. You need time to think through new claims or proposals being
   put forward by the other party.

5. You would like the other party to give proper consideration to
   your new proposal or concession.

6. You notice that the conflict is escalating and you need a 'cooling
   off' period.

7. You need to get approval for a decision from your constituents;
   or you need to get their viewpoint.

8. The discussion has been going on for too long and everybody is
   getting hungry and tired. You need a break.

9. You feel it may be useful to provide an opportunity for informal,
   exploratory talks with the other party, away from the bargaining
   table.

Who should call an adjournment?

The time to call for an adjournment is when the need first becomes
apparent. Failure to do so for fear it may be perceived as a
disruption or a waste of time by the other party is self-defeating.

Always summarize progress made so far before leaving the
negotiation room. Recapping is especially important in negotiations
where topics discussed are complex. Following the summary, get
explicit agreement on what you and the other party will discuss in
the next meeting. Otherwise, the other may well succumb to a
temptation to start over from the beginning or reopen the discussion
of an item that has already been settled.

Key points for building understanding

1. Never accept a first proposal.
2. Talk less not more. Listen. Ask questions.
3. Always remember your basic interests. List and place these at the front of your negotiation.
4. Use adjournments to keep control over your team and discussions.
5. Try 'bargaining by objectives': set yourself a clear, specific and realistic goal before entering a meeting. For instance, decide which information you would like to get from the other party. Adjourn as soon as this goal has been met. Then establish a new goal for the next meeting.
6. Summarize regularly. List the points of explanation, interpretation and understanding.
7. Do not use weak language, such as 'We hope', 'We like' and 'We prefer'. Say 'We need', 'We must have' or 'We require'.
8. Avoid emotional outbursts, blaming, personal attacks, sarcasm, point-scoring, interrupting and being 'too clever'. Practise signalling, questioning, paraphrasing, using humour, building rapport and remaining silent.

Finally, remember that the need for an adjournment is not negotiable. There is no need to ask permission for an adjournment. You have but to announce that you need time to adjourn and leave the bargaining table.

Step 5: Bargaining

In its purest form, it is mind pitted against mind. (John Illich, 1980)
It is better to give away the wool than the sheep. (Italian proverb)

This phase can also be separated into three components:

1. Getting and making concessions.
2. Breaking deadlocks.
3. Moving towards an agreement.

(1) Getting and making concessions

A concession is a revision of a previous position you have held and justified publicly. Concessions are always expected in negotiation, but the parties nevertheless try to move as little as possible.

Any concession presents you with three problems:

1. Should I make it now?
2. How much ground should I give?
3. What am I going to get in return?

How can you deal with these problems?

There are a number of approaches you can use to deal with these problems. One approach is to make conditional offers. By attaching conditions to your concessions, you get something for something rather than something for nothing. So whenever possible look for something in return for every move you think of making.

What else can you do to make effective concessions?

First, when making conditional offers, introduce the condition first and do not give details of the concessions until the other party shows some willingness to negotiate on the condition.

In addition, when considering concessions, keep in mind that:

- A good concession usually is a small one. Major shifts make it difficult for the negotiator to maintain a credible position and will almost certainly encourage further pressure from the other party to move even more.

- Concessions offered without specific pressure being applied are not worth much. They should be accepted, but only as a stepping stone for others.

- You may sometimes be in a position where you have little or no room to manoeuvre; but generally, it is courting disaster to go into any negotiation with no concession in mind or possible.

- One of the skills in negotiation is dealing with package claims, particularly in re-sorting them to get past 'road-blocks' and make satisfactory settlements possible.

- You should always try to promote in the other party a willingness to make concessions. You can do this by:
  - Convincing them that they cannot hold to their present position.
  - Showing them how they can move without loss of face.
  - Indicating that you too will move at some time.

Key points for managing your concession-making

In order to avoid unwise concessions (and agreements):

1. Know exactly where you intend to stop conceding.
2. Help the other party to concede by providing a rationale. Avoid loss of face.
3. When the other party makes a concession, repeat aloud their offer.
4. Offer your concessions tentatively. Use hypothetical questions, such as 'What would you say if I were to . . .?'.
5. Trade concessions. Make conditional offers. Use 'IF . . . THEN'.
6. Use packages to make concessions work for your objectives. Link issues.
7. Always value your concession in the other party's terms. Think and say what your concession is worth to them.
8. Never make concessions without thinking through the long-term consequences for yourself.
9. State your reasoning first, then make your concession.
10. Be firm on basic interests; be flexible on positions.

(2) Breaking deadlocks

As part of planning for negotiation, it is essential to think about the situation which would occur if the negotiations failed to achieve agreement.

Why do deadlocks arise?

Deadlock or stalemate can arise for a number of reasons, including the following:

- Both parties have widely divergent objectives.
- One party mistakes firmness for rigidity and will not make concessions even to keep the negotiation 'alive'.
- As a deliberate tactic during a negotiation to force the other party to reconsider its position and make concessions.

How do you handle deadlocks?

It is unwise to allow a negotiation to fail if the probable outcome, whether because of action by the other party or through third-party intervention, is worse than the position reached when breakdown occurs.

Several devices can be used to break a deadlock in negotiations, such as promises of future negotiations on a related topic, or making the introduction of a new condition subject to later review.

However, the main options for handling deadlocks are to take unilateral action to enforce an outcome, or to seek third-party intervention.

What types of third-party intervention are there?

The least extreme form of third-party assistance is **conciliation**, in which a conciliator works with the two parties to help them reach agreement.

Mediation is a more direct form of help. Here both parties agree to consider (but are bound to accept) a solution suggested by the outsider.

Arbitration is the most powerful and risky form of third-party intervention. This is where both parties bind themselves in advance to accept the third-party's solution.

Suggestions for breaking deadlocks

1. **Go back to information gathering** and building understanding to generate additional options. There may be an underlying issue that is not being addressed.

2. Try to **discover the barriers to effective negotiating.** Make a direct appeal to the other party. For instance 'Can you tell me why we are having so much trouble finding an acceptable solution?'.

3. **Agree not to agree** for the time being. Create time to reflect on the problem and resume negotiations later. Ask if more information is needed.

4. Inform the other party of the **consequences of failure** to reach a negotiated solution.

5. See if the other party is willing to **try out one of the proposed solutions** for a period of time.

6. **Call in an outside party** to act as a conciliator, a mediator or an arbitrator.

(3) Moving towards agreements

The purpose of negotiation is to reach agreement, not to score points in argument. However, in most circumstances, quick settlements should be avoided. They tend to result in extreme outcomes (high or low) and favour the more experienced negotiator.

The closer a negotiation is to reaching agreement, the more sensitively the discussion needs to be handled.

What tactics can be used to facilitate progress towards agreement?
A variety of tactics can be used. The most common techniques are:

- **Advice and suggestions**. For example 'You may be able to deal with this issue by . . .', 'The disadvantage of that is . . .'.

- **Promises** to indicate that compliance with what you want will benefit the other party. For example 'If you give us . . . then we may be able to help you with . . .'.

- **Threats** to indicate that failure to comply with your wishes will have adverse consequences as far as the other party is concerned. For example 'If you do this . . . then we shall be forced to . . .'.

- **Explanations** to tell the other party exactly why you want him/her to take certain actions. For example, their effects on organizational performance and on other people within the organization.

- **Praise** to let the other party know what kinds of things you value and therefore are likely to be appreciated in future. For example 'I think that was a valuable comment . . .', 'We appreciate your frankness . . .'.

- **Criticism** to let the other party know that you are highly dissatisfied with his/her behaviour. For example 'Please do not interrupt me'.

- **Leading questions** to gain compliance or acceptance by signalling quite clearly the response which the other party is expected to give. For example 'You must agree that . . .', 'Don't you think that . . .', 'You do see the point why . . .'.

- **Apologies** can help to stop a 'perceived' emotion inhibiting rational discussion, particularly if combined with a constructive discussion of ways of avoiding similar reactions in future. For example 'First of all I must apologize for . . .', 'I'm very sorry, I didn't realize'.

- **Reflecting** allows the emotion to burn itself out by reflecting back the emotional content of what the other person is saying, in a concerned and non-evaluative way. For example 'You seem upset about . . .', 'You feel it would be unfair to . . .'.

- **Adjournments** are probably more useful than any other technique as a means of handling high emotion.

- **Humour,** or good-natured banter, can be used to reduce tension and help create a bond between the parties.

- Periodic, **joint agreed summaries** of progress can secure a phased agreement and prevent reversion to earlier argument.

- **Proposals** may initially be put as hypothetical suggestions. This makes it easier for both parties to avoid the pressure of immediate acceptance or withdrawal. Remember that fear of losing face can severely inhibit progress. So, there is a positive advantage in making it easy for the other side to move, rather than challenging them on a win–lose basis. Remember also that proposals are best sold on their advantages to the other party, not to your own benefits.

BODY LANGUAGE IN NEGOTIATION

A lot of information in negotiations is communicated non-verbally through the body language of the individual negotiators. Some of these non-verbal signals are easy to read. For instance, it is obvious that when people smile, unbutton their collars, or take their jacket off, they are beginning to feel comfortable in your presence. Less obvious gestures include moving closer to you, crossing arms and speaking slowly. Skilled negotiators are aware of this and use body language consciously to influence the other party's response to their arguments and suggestions.

Some of the attitudes and behaviours revealed by body language are:

Active listening:	– Eyes wide and alert
	– Leaning slightly forward
	– Hands open and arms extended
Defensiveness:	– Eyes open and alert
	– Erect body
	– Arms and legs tightly crossed
	– Fists clenched
Frustration:	– Tightly clenched hands
	– Rubbing the nape of the neck
	– Looking at the exit or outside
Boredom:	– Leaning backwards
	– Looking at one's watch
	– Doodling or drumming fingers
Confidence:	– Relaxed and expansive gestures
	– Sitting upright
Deception:	– Minimal eye contact
	– Sudden changes in voice pitch
	– Covering the mouth while talking

Step 6: Closing

Nothing is settled until it is settled right. (L.D. Brandeis, 1856–1941)

Normally, the closing phase of a negotiation comprises three stages:

1. Formulating an agreement.
2. Ensuring implementation.
3. Reviewing your negotiating experience.

(1) Formulating an agreement

To get an agreement, the other party needs to be convinced that s/he cannot push you any further. S/he may believe this if:

- Your final offer is tabled with conviction.
- Your final offer is not seen as yet another in a chain of final offers.
- The nature of your concessions has become minimal and they are being won with increasing difficulty.
- Your previous willingness to move is no longer apparent despite pressure being applied.
- You suggest that the other party refers your 'final offer' to his/her members for consideration.

How do you make final offers?

- Your final offer and agreement needs to be timed to coincide with a period of constructive discussion – not during a combative phase.
- It is important to achieve credibility for any statement about an offer being final – the tone and style of such a statement may be as important as its substance.

How to formulate an agreement?

Before formulating an agreement, check that all aspects have been agreed, particularly dates for implementation, review or completion, and definitions of terms.

Ensure full understanding of what has been agreed by final summaries and by producing written confirmation. Some record of the outcome of negotiations, however informal, is desirable.

Unresolved issues should not be 'fudged' by producing vague or ambiguous forms of words in order to achieve apparent agreement.

Keep in mind that sound closing of negotiation is never done in a hurry. Quicker is rarely better.

How can you identify a 'good deal'?

Regardless of what is agreed, both parties will always express their satisfaction with the final deal.

You should expect the other party to 'broadcast' their satisfaction with the deal to which s/he has agreed (as you no doubt will yourself!) to show to those s/he represents that a good job has been done on their behalf. S/he is judged and rewarded by them on what is 'delivered'.

While it is perfectly possible to have a win–lose finish, there is little doubt that the successful negotiator aims for one which can be described as win–win.

While both parties may win, it is rarely a 50/50 split finish. The better share goes either to the party which has the power, and knows how to use it, or the party which plans and conducts its negotiation better, when power is equal.

GAMES NEGOTIATORS PLAY

According to Acuff and Villere (1976) much of the delay in settling disputes is attributable to games negotiators play. 'Game' is defined in terms of transactional analysis (TA). The following eight games appear to be typical in a multitude of negotiating settings.

(1) Expertise

The purpose of this game is to give the impression one's homework has been done by establishing at the beginning of the negotiation that one has a knowledge of the facts.

(2) Snow job

This game is similar to 'Expertise' in that facts and figures are used to overwhelm the other.

(3) So what

This game is played by negotiators immediately after a concession has been made. Regardless of the importance of the concession, the receiver's posture is that the item really was not important in the first place. In other words 'What you gave me is small potatoes,now let's get on to the biggies'.

(4) Wheat and chaff
This is played by putting in chaff (minutiae or not really priority items) in order to obtain the wheat (priority items). The idea is to pad the demands with items you can easily give away.

(5) Wooden leg
The argument here is that one is suffering from a limitation that makes further movement impossible. A popular wooden leg is the lack of financial resources or the inflexibility of constituents.

(6) Sandbagger
In this game, one party tries to negotiate from a position of strength by establishing his/her own weakness. For example, s/he may claim that negotiating is a new experience, and ask for the other party's sympathy, patience and understanding.

(7) Boredom
In this game, body language is used to notify the other party that their points fail to impress. This game is best played during a time when the other side is making their most salient and forceful points.

(8) Yes . . . but . . .
Every time a solution is suggested, the other party derides it with a 'Yes . . . but . . .'. For example 'We very much feel the need to negotiate this week, but our schedule looks awfully tight. Any suggestions as to when to get together?'.

(2) Securing implementation

An agreement is not successful until it has been effectively implemented. It is therefore often helpful to include an implementation programme as an integral part of a negotiated agreement. Such a programme will define what has to be done, when and by whom.

How to implement agreements?
For some agreements, implementation may be best effected by a joint team.

Those affected by, or required to apply, an agreement need adequate information and explanation, even though they are not involved in the actual negotiation.

This communication should be based on defining who needs to know what, how and by whom this information should be given and by what methods and to what time-scales.

Key points for closing the negotiation

> To avoid unpleasant surprises, before adjourning the last round of discussions:
>
> 1. Clarify the terms of the agreement.
> 2. Ask yourself the question: WHO gets HOW MUCH, of WHAT, WHEN?
> 3. Try to get the agreement in writing.
> 4. If the agreement is oral, send a written note to the other party listing the points of agreement, disagreement, interpretation and clarification as you see them. Do this as soon as possible after the meeting.

(3) Reviewing your negotiating experience

After closing the negotiation, you should review your experience. Ask yourself the following questions:

- How satisfied are you with the outcome of the negotiations?
- Who was the most effective negotiator? Who conceded most?
- What strategies and actions helped the discussions most?
- What actions hindered the discussion?
- Did you trust the other party? What affected this feeling most?
- How well was time used? Could it be used better?
- How well did people listen to each other? Who talked most?
- Were creative solutions suggested? What happened to them?
- Did you have a good understanding of the underlying issues and concerns of the other party? Did the other party understand yours?
- How adequate was your preparation? How did this affect the negotiation?
- What were the strongest arguments put forward by the other party? How receptive was the other party to your arguments and ideas?
- What are your main learning points from this negotiation? What would you do differently next time?

REVIEW QUESTIONS

1. Think of a situation at work where you will need to negotiate in the near future.

- How would you determine your range of objectives?
- What is your BATNA?
- How will this affect your power in the negotiation?

2. Looking at your scores on the Thomas Kilmann questionnaire:

- What is your preferred negotiating style?
- Think of a situation where the other four styles would be more appropriate.
- What steps do you need to take to develop the style with the lowest score?

3. Think of a negotiation you were involved in over the last few weeks.

- Which negotiation tactics did you use?
- How effective were these tactics in achieving your objectives?
- Looking through the list of tactics described in this book, pick out two or three negotiation tactics which you would use in a similar situation next time you negotiate.

4. Listed below are a number of 'dirty tactics' sometimes used in negotiation. You should be prepared to counter these. For each tactic, decide how you could counter it when used to influence you.

- Appeal to particular norms concerning equality, fairness and justice.
- Threaten with deadlock, strike or reprisals.
- Remain silent; fail to respond.
- Nibble; make incremental demands, piece-by piece.
- Set a deadline.
- Make a 'final' offer.
- Use personal attacks.
- Change negotiator(s) during the talks.
- Suggest splitting the difference between two proposals.
- Inundate you with information.
- Adopt a good guy/bad guy routine.
- Re-open previously settled issues.
- Show a lack of goodwill/sincerity.

- Act aggressively.
- Make 'take it or leave it' offers.

5. Considering the key points for the negotiation listed in Steps 3 and 4:

- How would you start your next negotiation?
- What would be three things you should do more of (or less of) to avoid emotional outbursts, blaming or interrupting the other party?

6. Described below are eight statements commonly used to block proposals. For each statement decide how you could respond using (reflective or open-ended) questions.

- Sounds good . . . but it will cost a lot of money!
- It's a great idea . . . but I don't think my boss will agree!
- I'd like to . . . but I can't take responsibility for this decision!
- Well, it's OK in theory . . . but our situation is different!
- We tried something like this three years ago . . . it didn't work!
- Why change? It's working all right now!
- It's not very practical. Think of the disruption it would cause!
- Come off it . . . let's get back to reality!

7. Think about a previous negotiation with your boss or subordinates where you feel you could have reached a better settlement. How did you 'make concessions' and 'move to agreement'? How might you do it more effectively next time you negotiate?

8. Identify two occasions at work or at home when body language has been helpful to you in negotiating? What habits of your own do you need to control and how might you do it?

CASE STUDY: THE TEMPERAMENTAL TALENT

Introduction
This case was written by Sheila Udall to illustrate the six-step approach to negotiation. After reading the case, ask yourself the following questions:

1. Did Chris have a clear strategy for the meeting with Mark? How effective was it?
2. Can you identify the different stages of the negotiation? What helped or hindered each one?
3. If you were to coach Chris in a similar situation, what do you think he did well? What could he have done differently and better in dealing with this situation?

Background

Vincent Randell is the Head of Personnel, at Jordan Tectonics, a small software engineering firm located in the North of England. Ten minutes ago he received a telephone call from **Chris Rosen**, the Head of Research and Development, who asked to see him urgently. Deeply concerned about the anger in Chris's voice, Vincent said to come over to his office immediately.

Chris explains the problem

'Hi Chris, what can I do for you? it seemed really important on the 'phone' said Vincent, greeting Chris into his office and inviting him to sit down.

'He's done it this time. He's really gone over the top. This will be impossible to sort out without a battle' yelled Chris, getting more and more agitated.

'OK, calm down and tell me about it. Who is *he*? asked Vincent.

'Sorry, it's Mark, you know our leading software designer, the person Frank was rattling on about at the meeting on Monday. I said I wanted a word about him, but things have just become impossible since then' replied Chris.

'So what's happened?' prompted Vincent.

'Well apparently last night Frank went down to the test room to remind Mark about a meeting today with a new client. Mark was at his terminal and without turning round said to Frank to wait a minute, then ignored Frank for 15 minutes. Frank suggested that he stopped 'playing'. Next they had a blazing row and Mark stormed out. What's worse, he's not in this morning and the meeting with the client has had to be rescheduled'.

'Is this the first time he's done something like that?' asked Vincent.

'Yes, well no, it's not the first time Mark has lost his temper. We've had some real battles in our time, but he's never taken it this far before' replied Chris.

'Has he missed client meetings before?' Vincent probed.

'Only once, when his mother was rushed into hospital. Maybe there are personal problems this time, though he has not said anything to me. The trouble is Frank is adamant saying we cannot have staff behaving like that and that Mark's got to go. I agree we can't have people behaving like that, but Mark is the brightest spark we've got. Everyone recognizes he's a genius. He's difficult, but we can't afford to lose him, and the opposition would grab him in an instant. Frank does not understand that.'

'How would other people, apart from Frank describe Mark?' asked Vincent.

Chris thought for a moment. 'Depends on who you talk to' he said. 'Most colleagues would see his good side. I find him hard to manage. He can be pretty temperamental, but I admire him. He is extremely able and dedicated. He may like playing computer games but he's the hardest working person in my department. He says he uses the games to "break free" when he is working on a really difficult problem. I can understand that but we have to get him to understand the pressures we are under.'

Vincent paused, then queried 'Have you tried talking to him before?'

'Yes, he says he loathes people looking over his shoulder. What he wants is a clear target and then to be left alone' replied Chris.

'Can you afford to lose him?' Vincent asked.

'Certainly not at the moment. I know our competitors are "courting" him.'

'How am I going to approach him, without making it worse?' Chris asked pensively. 'I must find a way of getting him to conform a bit, without losing his commitment.'

Vincent smiled. 'Well let's think it through, clearly you will need to be well prepared when you talk to him. We cannot afford to go wrong this time.'

Immediately after his discussion with Vincent, Chris went back to his office to think about how to approach Mark. He knew he needed to be careful and plan his approach. He certainly did not want another battle. By nature he was not a particularly forceful person. He preferred to work 'with' people rather than fight them, but he knew he easily lost his temper when things did not go his way.

Chris wondered about the reason for Mark's non-appearance at work that day. He knew Mark lived alone, but spent quite a lot of time with his family. He wondered if this could be the reason for his absence.

He decided to call Mark into his office as soon as he came in, find out why he had missed work and sort the situation out once and for all.

Mark explains his absence
Two days after speaking to Vincent, Mark was back at work. Chris called him straight away.

'Hi Mark, glad you are back. Can we have a word this morning some time?'

'Is it urgent?' Mark replied quickly. 'I'm just about to start on the revision of the P70 spec.'

'Yes, it's urgent and it will only take about half an hour. Can you come at 9.30?'

'Hey, sounds serious. Not going to sack me are you?' laughed Mark.

'Certainly not' replied Chris shortly. 'Look, I need to speak to you about a number of things, the other night in particular. Just get up here at 9.30, OK?'

It wasn't meant to be threatening. However, as he hung up the phone, Chris realized he was getting upset again. He took the opportunity to grab a cup of coffee, and plan the meeting. By the time Mark arrived he was ready to talk business.

'Hello, Mark. Thanks for coming up. Take a seat.'

Mark sat down, looking a little uneasy.

'As I said on the phone there are a number of things I'd like to talk with you about. We have about half an hour. Is that OK?'

'Sure. What's going on?'

'Well, first, I know you have been off for the last two days. We need to talk about that. Secondly, I would like to know what happened the evening before you went away. And lastly something important happened whilst you were gone.'

Chris was pleased he sounded so calm.

'No problem' Mark replied and he added quickly 'but there is something I wanted to talk about to you about too'.

'Something serious?' Chris enquired tentatively.

'Yes, I've been to see the new factory of Thomson Electronics. That's why I took off. Well I had some holiday owing, and there was nothing crucial on here. So when Tom, a friend who works there, asked if I'd like to see the set up, I jumped at it. Thought you wouldn't mind' Mark added.

Chris replied 'Well I'm certainly interested in that, but perhaps we could come back to it later. Nothing crucial on here you said. Are you sure?'.

'Yeah. I had just cracked the final bug on the Roberts project and had not started on the P70. Why?'

Chris took a deep breath. 'What about the meeting with Rawley Manufacturing?'

Mark looked surprised. 'Oh that' he said. 'I wasn't involved. Why do you mention it?'

'You were not involved?' Chris asked.

'No. When I last spoke to Stephen Bennett's assistant, he said he would get back to me if I was needed. He didn't, so I assumed they could handle it without me.'

Chris made a mental note to check with Stephen, and went on. 'OK, would you like to tell me about the evening before you went off?'

'What about it?' retorted Mark.

'Did you see Frank Edwards?'

Mark nodded.

Chris went on. 'What happened?'

'Well, he arrived in the middle of the final test. I asked him to wait whilst I checked the results. After only a couple of minutes he interrupted me saying "stop fiddling; I need some information for the management accounts". When I said I had just solved a major puzzle he yelled "you're always playing at something". I yelled back and it kind of got out of hand.'

Mark sat for a moment, then continued 'I realized how tired I was, so when Tom rang to invite me over to see his new plant I decided to take off'.

Chris looked thoughtful. 'You were tired and so decided on the spur of the moment to visit a friend?'

'Well in fairness, he asked me to go work for his company.'

Chris felt a sudden shock. 'Are you considering it?' he asked nervously. His expression showed that he almost did not want to know the answer.

'I'd be daft not to' replied Mark swiftly.

The silence seemed eternal, until Chris took a deep breath and said 'Well in that case I think this talk needs longer than we can spare right now. We need to sort out exactly what happened the other day. I'm not happy about staff getting into a row with the Financial Director, and if you are considering moving to another company, there's a lot to discuss. How about meeting here, tomorrow morning same time?'.

'Fine with me' replied Mark without much conviction, 'See you then'.

As Mark left the office Chris sat back. 'I need to plan the next stage very carefully' he thought. The company could not afford to lose Mark, given the amount of work that was coming up. Mark had always shown enormous commitment to the company. He worked long hours, never gave up on a problem and showed real interest in the projects they were working on. His colleagues enjoyed his slightly off-beat sense of humour and certainly appreciated his talent. 'I can understand Mark's position about being left alone to get on with the job' Chris thought. On the other hand, Mark's manner with Frank Edwards was out of order. Rows with the Financial Director were less than helpful, and missing meetings with important clients, without a word to anyone, was simply not acceptable. 'I must get Mark to see that if he wants to progress in the company (or any company for that matter) he simply cannot treat important people in such a cavalier fashion.'

The following morning.

Chris stood up as Mark walked into his office.

'Hi Mark, take a seat, thanks for coming. We have more time this morning, so I'd like to talk more about your plans to leave. OK?'

'Fine, go ahead' said Mark settling into his seat.

Chris smiled back. 'Tell me more about your visit to the Thomson factory' he said.

Mark leaned forward. 'It's a really interesting project, sorting out the new CI system, and it would be all my responsibility. It's a great opportunity to expand my experience.'

'Is that what you are looking for, to develop experience in these new CI systems?' Chris asked.

'Yes, I like working with you but the rest of the company don't seem to understand what we do. It's different at Thomsons, and this project has a deadline of nine months. They are under a lot of pressure.'

'What about after nine months?' Chris enquired.

Mark looked thoughtful. 'I'm not really sure what would happen after this project was completed' he said.

'What about the salary? Would it be more that here?' posed Chris.

'Yes, the money's good.'

'So, the work would be really interesting for nine months, with an increase in salary, but it would mean moving or a new car and you are not sure what would happen after the project is done?'

Mark nodded.

'I can understand the challenge being appealing' Chris continued 'but would you really be better off? What if we could develop your involvement in the CI project here? I am sure we can sort the issues with Frank'.

'Could I get into CI here?' asked Mark.

'Well I can't promise, but we could explore it with Personnel. I know Vincent has ideas how we should broaden our base of experience. And it's something Frank Edwards is really keen on' Chris replied.

Mark sounded enthusiastic. 'I'd really like that' he said. 'I think I'd prefer to stay, if Frank is not on my back. He's really got it in for me, you know. It feels like being spied on. Suddenly you look round and he's there again. That's the big attraction of Thomsons. I'd really be my own boss.'

'You will have to sort that out with him directly' Chris pointed out. 'But if you BOTH get a better understanding of each other's priorities, I'm sure it will work.'

Mark smiled, so Chris continued. 'If you won't pursue going to Thomsons I will talk to Vincent about opportunities to get you on CI work. What do you say?'

'Sounds good, but let me think about it. I'll talk to Tom right away, and let you know my decision after the weekend. Is that OK with you?'

Chris smiled. 'Great, thanks, and I'll have a word with Frank by next week. I'm sure we can work something out.'

'Perhaps we can talk about that some more after the meeting' Mark replied. 'Thanks for your time. I really appreciate your help.'

Chris drew a deep sigh of relief as Mark rose and left the office.

3

Negotiating within groups

If a house be divided against itself, that house cannot stand.
(New Testament, Mark 3:25)

In many organizations, negotiating is increasingly seen as a useful and even necessary skill for effective teamwork and decision making in groups. Whereas in the past many decisions were made by individuals who expected other people to implement them, nowadays economic and social pressures demand a more participative style of working and managing. Initiatives such as total quality management and empowerment encourage staff at all levels to become involved in a wide variety of situations where joint agreement through negotiating is necessary. In these situations, the rules and guidelines of interpersonal negotiation may be of little help because they fail to capture the complexity of the group processes. These complexities are most apparent when the parties have to reach a consensus agreement on issues or interests which cannot easily be reconciled.

In this chapter, we look at four related processes that affect the dynamics and outcome of negotiating in groups:

1. Organizing successful meetings.
2. Communicating with impact.
3. Identifying creative solutions.
4. Achieving consensus.

Organizing a successful meeting

> If a problem causes many meetings, the meetings eventually become more important than the problem. (Arthur Bloch, Murphy's Law, 1977)

Research shows that managers spend as much as 30 per cent of their time in meetings, while top management spends closer to 50 per cent. These figures emphasize the importance of good 'meeting management' skills. Since managers spend so much time in meetings, their own success is to a large extent determined by how effectively those meetings are managed.

How can you make meetings effective?

Whetten and Cameron (1991) identified the following pointers for managers who want to increase their effectiveness as team leaders.

(1) Specify the purpose of the meeting
Before scheduling a meeting, ask yourself 'Is a meeting the most appropriate means for communicating?'. It is sometimes more practical and efficient to communicate in other ways. For example, do not call a meeting when the information can be conveyed by telephone or fax or when some of the key people cannot attend. However, do call a meeting when:

- There are some complex problems that require extensive information sharing and discussion.
- You need to build commitment among the group members to a chosen course of action.
- The chosen audience needs to get, as far as is possible, the same message at the same time.

(2) Invite individuals with the appropriate knowledge and orientation
Effective groups typically contain some members who are highly task oriented and others who are concerned about maintaining the quality of the group's process. Meetings that are dominated by task-oriented people tend to be very efficient, but at the expense of group cohesion and individual commitment. In contrast, groups that are dominated by process-oriented people tend to err in favour of encouraging everyone to participate, even if some have little to

contribute. Thus, it is usually a good idea to have both task- and process-orientated members in the group.

(3) Ensure the size of the group is compatible with the task
A common mistake when planning a meeting is to invite too many people, thinking that it is important to input from as many minds as possible. The result can be a superficial discussion of a wide range of issues, rather than a focused discussion of the key issues. Also, some people prefer not to contribute if the group is too large.

(4) Manage the process of the meeting
To avoid unproductive discussions and wasting valuable time, remember to:

- Present and clarify the overall purpose of the meeting, specify the target length of time for it, and highlight specific agenda items.

- Allow people to introduce themselves, if necessary, and make them feel comfortable with one another.

- Establish process 'ground rules', such as how decisions will be made, how much time should be spent in discussing an issue before making a decision, and how to deal with issues on which there is no agreement.

Avoiding some common pitfalls in group meetings

1. When critical thinking is important, **avoid 'groupthink'** by refraining from expressing strong opinions during the idea-generating phase of the discussions.

2. Counteract the tendency for groups to make more risky decisions than individuals, by holding every member of the group personally responsible for the group's final decision. **Prevent 'diffusion of responsibility'.**

3. People tend to adopt a more extreme position after a group discussion than they held prior to the meeting. To **reduce this 'polarization'**, ask every member of the group to think through the major issues before the meeting.

4. **Block efforts to divert the discussion.** In poorly managed meetings, individuals can easily divert the discussion from common issues to personal concerns. As a result, the meeting turns into a staged political debate in which antagonists try to enhance their personal status in the group, and/or win allies, rather than solve problems.

- As early as possible, get a report from each person with a specific task. This reinforces the principle of accountability and provides public recognition for the presenter.

- Manage the meeting to achieve equitable participation. Prevent the domination of single members or points of view.

- Close the meeting by summarizing what has been decided and by reviewing assignments and timings for the next meetings, if necessary.

Additional tips for improving the quality and effectiveness of meetings are provided in the Appendix.

Communicating with impact

How well we communicate is determined not by how well we say things but by how well we are understood. (Andrew S. Grove, CEO Intel Corporation, 1987)

One of the most discouraging experiences in team negotiations is the sense of not being understood. When this happens, it results in frustration and confrontation. Neither person hears the other one. They play a semantic game of ping-pong in which words, not meanings, are exchanged.

When and why does communication go wrong?
In group negotiations, the communication process is often frustrated or blocked when one or more of the parties use 'high-risk' responses. These responses include:

- Ordering the others to do something, or to stop doing something important.

- Threatening, alluding to the use of force.

- Moralizing, putting a halo around your own solution.

- Judging, criticizing, making negative evaluations of the other party.

- Name-calling, stereotyping, making the others feel stupid or foolish.

- Diagnosing, explaining why you think somebody in the group is behaving as s/he is.
- Diverting, pushing the problem of the other party away.

What generally happens when individuals experience high-risk responses in group negotiations?

There are at least seven changes which can commonly occur.

1. These responses are usually experienced by the others as ploys to derail the negotiation, lower their self-esteem, distance them from the real problem, or take responsibility away from the group. They cause resentment or defensiveness and therefore provoke an aggressive response.

2. Face-saving concerns increase. In the early stages of the discussion, the parties are simply out to do as well as they can for themselves, with little concern for how well or poorly the others are doing. As conflict escalates, however, this 'individualistic' orientation is replaced by competition. Now doing well means outdoing the others or, if one is experiencing a loss, making sure that no one else does better than oneself.

3. As conflict escalates, gentle tactics to persuade the others (persuasive arguments, promises) are replaced by 'heavier' behaviours: threats, personal attacks and so on. The group atmosphere changes from one of relaxed, unhurried consideration of problems to one of tension and competition.

4. Group members begin to see only the best in their own position and the worst in that of the other group members. Inaccurate and uncomplimentary stereotypes form. Judgements are made about individuals on the basis of bargaining positions, not on the basis of accurate knowledge and information.

5. Small, specific issues give way to larger, more general issues, and there is a general deterioration in the communication between the participants. People tend to hear only that which supports their position. They do not see the similarities; they see only the differences in positions.

6. Loyalty to the total group decreases and allegiances within the group are formed. Any person who preaches moderation or tact or 'softness' in dealing with each other is likely to be confronted with pressure to change his/her viewpoint.

7. The style of leadership changes. More autocracy is accepted. The chairperson is given much more freedom to act unilaterally. No group decision is found.

So what can be done to make your communication more effective?

There are a number of basic rules that can help make your communications more effective. The following five are among the most important:

(1) Bear in mind that communication is a two-way process
People communicate with (not to) people. So before you start to communicate, take time to discover what arouses the others' enthusiasm, what stirs their interest, what leaves them cold and indifferent, what annoys them and makes them touchy, and where their blind spots are.

(2) Know precisely what you want to say
However, be careful of how the others are likely to interpret and react to your objectives. Remember that the other negotiators always have two questions in mind 'How will this negotiation affect me?' and 'What's in it for me?'.

(3) Remind yourself that how you say something is often more important than what you say
If other people do not accept your manner, they will probably not accept your message. So be conscious that you communicate with your words, body posture, facial expressions, tone of voice and inflections.

(4) Look at the other person when you talk to him/her
Try to get rid of things like nervous actions and anything else that might distract a listener from concentrating on what you are saying.

(5) The way you organize your messages strongly affect their impact
The tips listed below tell you how to do this better.

TWELVE TIPS FOR MAKING YOUR COMMUNICATION MORE EFFECTIVE

1. **Use two-sided arguments** and present your side last.
2. In most cases, it is helpful to **state the conclusions of your argument**. If, however, you are dealing with a highly intelligent audience, and you can offer convincing arguments, it is better to let them draw their own conclusions.

3. **Phrase your argument in the same 'language'** (words and expressions) used by the audience.

4. **Avoid using inflammatory adjectives** such as 'good', 'bad', 'unreasonable', 'outrageous' and 'unfair'. They are not specific and open the door to unnecessary arguments about what is fair, reasonable and so forth.

5. **Avoid using generalizations.** The words 'always', 'never' and 'constantly' are value judgements and imply that there are no exceptions to what you are saying.

6. **Tailor your argument to your intended audience.** Appeals to religious values may be very persuasive for some people, but ineffective with people who do not have strong religious beliefs.

7. **Keep it short and simple.** Avoid verbal diarrhoea. Most arguments are far more effective when they are cut by at least half. Get to your point quickly and confidently without rambling.

8. **Avoid argument dilution.** One strong argument has more persuasive power than ten weak ones. Similarly, do not surround your best arguments with tangential arguments or a lot of details.

9. **Put your strongest arguments first** if you want to convince or interest people who are not involved. Arguments that come in the middle of a presentation are hardest to remember.

10. **Ask open questions** ('Why? Where? When?') and hypothetical questions ('What if?'). These can help reveal how other people are thinking and feeling. Remember that the language of feelings and emotions is often far more compelling than intellectual argument.

11. **Make your arguments and questions logical and coherent.** Questions should follow in a logical sequence and not ask for more than one piece of information at a time.

12. If possible, get other people to restate your ideas and conclusions for themselves. **Encourage active participation.**

Looking for creative solutions

Discovery of a solution consists of looking at the same thing as everyone else and thinking something different. (Albert Szent-Gyorgyi, 1983)

What are the advantages of group problem solving?
Given even a minimal level of trust and goodwill, group problem solving can have a number of advantages. They include:

1. Being capable of generating a greater quantity and variety of ideas than the average individual.

2. Enabling group members to be 'irreverent', to hear a variety of viewpoints and to challenge old absolutes.

3. People usually are more committed to a solution when they have been given a fair opportunity to participate in its development and are aware of all the factors underlying its existence.

What are the pitfalls?

Although groups can be effective at problem solving and finding creative solutions there are a number of pitfalls, including:

- The solutions devised by groups are often dismissed by those in positions of influence as sub-optimal. Some types of group (such as working parties and committees) have a well-earned reputation for abysmal decisions.

- All too often, participants learn that what appears to be a fair, democratic process is really a charade in which decisions have already been made by those in power and group involvement is used as a means of placating those who have to live with the decision.

- People are often appointed to groups (or volunteer) for a variety of inappropriate (political) reasons.

- Very few people are trained in the art of creative problem solving and the effective use of group members, which can result in a rapid deterioration of both the process and the morale of those involved.

- Unless well managed, a group effort at creative problem solving can be a colossal waste of time, money and effort.

So what can be done to improve the group's problem-solving skills?

We suggest three major approaches:

1. Preventing groupthink
2. Structuring the problem-solving process
3. Using special techniques for creating novel ideas

Let us consider each approach in turn.

(1)　Preventing 'groupthink'

A widely documented pitfall in group decision making is that the pressure to reach a consensus interferes with critical thinking. Irving Janis (1982), a prominent social psychologist, has conducted extensive research on this phenomenon. Specifically, in examining historic foreign policy fiascos, he observed that most were made by groups exhibiting the following eight characteristics:

1. **Illusion of invulnerability**: The group feels sure that its past successes will continue.

2. **Shared stereotypes**: The group members dismiss disconfirming information by discrediting its source ('lawyers are needlessly conservative').

3. **Rationalization**: Members rationalize away threats to an emerging consensus.

4. **Illusion of morality**: Members believe that they, as moral individuals, are not likely to make bad decisions.

5. **Self-censorship**: Individuals keep silent about misgivings and try to minimize their doubts.

6. **Direct pressure**: Sanctions are imposed on members who explore deviant viewpoints.

7. **Mind-guarding**: Certain individuals (gatekeepers) protect the group from being exposed to disturbing ideas.

8. **Illusion of unanimity**: The group members conclude that they have reached a consensus because the most vocal members are in agreement.

To avoid these problems, take the following precautions:

• Make clear to every group member that it is creativity, not unanimity, that is valued.

• The chairperson or group leader should avoid stating his/her personal preference among the alternatives being considered.

• At intervals, break the group into sub-groups, each considering the same issues.

• If possible, use outside experts as sounding boards and devil's advocates.

(2)　Structuring the problem-solving process

Another common pitfall in group decision making is to choose the first satisfactory solution proposed, without considering possible alternatives. Given this tendency, a structured approach to decision making is usually needed to search for creative solutions. This approach can be achieved as follows:

- *Ask whether there really is a conflict of interest.* An apparent conflict of interest between the members of the group may be an illusion.

- If there is a real conflict of interests, *define the conflict in terms of underlying interests.* Ask the participants why they think the issue is important. The point is that interests can often be organized into hierarchical trees, with more basic interests underpinning more superficial ones.

- *Identify and agree the criteria* that will be used to evaluate potential solutions to the conflict. This step is often overlooked because of the parties' enthusiasm for dealing with the content of the issues.

- *Decide what will happen* if none of the identified options is acceptable. For example, who will make the final decision?

- *Generate as many options for solutions as possible,* brainstorm and clarify as necessary. Ask hypothetical questions.

- *Evaluate the available options* against the criteria and decide on the best option or combination of options. Test any selected options to make sure they satisfy the parties' needs.

- *Decide* specifically *who does what, and when.* Build individual accountability into the action or implementation plan for the decision.

(3) Special techniques for generating novel ideas in groups
Most people have trouble solving problems creatively. Over the years, they have built up certain conceptual blocks or models that inhibit them from finding novel solutions. These blocks are largely unrecognized and unconscious, so the only way to improve creative problem solving is to use techniques and methods that help to overcome them.

How can you enhance people's creativity in group problem solving?
You may try the following five methods:

(1) Ask the group members to discuss the issues via analogies
This forces them to think about the conflict in terms of its similarity to other, unrelated disputes or conflicts. If two conflicts are similar

in some respects, it is very likely that they are similar in others. So an analogy may suggest new approaches to solving the issues.

(2)   Ask the group members to reverse roles
This forces them to think about the issues from the other person's viewpoint. By arguing the issues from another vantage point, negotiators may get new insights and be induced to give up a cherished, but impractical, position.

(3)   Use the 'nominal group technique'
This has two stages. First, group members work individually to generate alternatives or decide on the best option. Then collectively they list and evaluate the plans, ideas or judgements that were generated in the first stage.

(4)   Use the 'round robin technique'
Here each individual writes the problem he or she has been given on the top of three 5-by-8-inch cards and then writes a possible solution on each card. After perhaps five minutes, each individual passes the cards to the next person, who writes a new solution or idea on each of the three cards. After everyone has had the opportunity to respond to all the problems, the cards are returned to the whole group, whose job it is to discuss the pros and cons of the various ideas and determine which option to adopt.

(5)   Work with a 'single negotiating text'
The essence of this procedure is to prepare a discussion paper which sets out the lines of a possible agreement. Then there are a series of sessions in which the parties prepare revised and improved versions of the document. Through the revisions and modifications, the document gradually becomes a single illustrative draft text of a complete agreement. The objective of the exercise is to improve the text until everyone believes it cannot be further improved. At that point the text is presented to the group for their acceptance or rejection, or otherwise to resolve any remaining points of disagreement.
This technique has a number of advantages:

- It avoids the otherwise overwhelming pressure on the parties to crystallize and harden their positions.

- It allows progress to be made without anyone having to make 'concessions'.

- It encourages commenting on, rather than criticizing, the ideas of the other parties.
- It keeps the negotiators' minds focused on the problem.
- In multilateral negotiations, like those over international trade agreements, such a procedure is almost mandatory if chaos is to be avoided.

Achieving consensus

Getting everybody to agree on stuff never did seem to work for me. (Milt Kuolt, founder Horizon Air Industries, 1988)

Reaching consensus is harder work than more mechanistic forms of decision making, such as voting or flipping a coin, but the investment in energy (expected to make the group function effectively without alienating its members) can have a dramatic pay-off.

How can you achieve consensus in groups?
Jones and Pfeiffer (1973) have made a number of suggestions about how consensus can be achieved within groups. The following are particularly relevant in team negotiation.

(1)   Clarify the concept
The main reason why consensus often fails is that usually people do not understand it. It is not a method that demands agreement by the total group. It simply requires that individuals be willing to go along with the groups' predominant view and carry out the implications of the decision in good faith.

(2)   Make the time and skills available to make it work
Without these, the group becomes highly vulnerable to domination or intimidation by a few and to political game playing by individuals unwilling to 'let go' of their personal agendas as the group moves toward a well-conceived decision.

(3)   Do not allow members to argue in order to win as individuals
What is 'right' is the best collective judgement of the group as a whole.

Key points for negotiating within groups

---

(1) Organizing successful meetings

- Determine if you need to attend or organize the meeting. Perhaps other methods of communication are more efficient.
- Make decisions regarding who and how many people to invite. Balance the composition of the group.
- Prepare and distribute an agenda before the meeting.
- Establish the ground rules of the discussion, such as how decisions will be made.
- Conclude the meeting by summarizing what was accomplished, reviewing assignments and making arrangements for later meetings, if necessary.

(2) Communicating with impact

- Take time to assess the audience. Find out what triggers their attention
- Be mindful of how others are likely to react to your message. Anticipate their concerns. Remember that manner is more important than meaning. Make your body language consistent with your verbal message.
- Structure your message to keep the others listening. Be brief and to the point. Avoid argument dilution. Summarize your argument.

(3) Identifying creative solutions

- Avoid groupthink.
- Structure the decision-making process.
- If necessary, work with a single negotiating text, or other techniques of fostering creative problem solving.

(4) Achieving consensus

- Clarify the concept.
- Provide the time and skills necessary to make it work.
- Do not allow some people to hijack the discussion.
- When appropriate, use other methods of decision making, such as voting.

---

(4)   Do not stifle innovation

Present conflict on ideas, solutions, predictions and so on as helping rather than hindering the process of seeking consensus. Assure each person that they have the right to question the process through which discussions are carried out and to stop the process when it is becoming ineffective.

(5) Watch out for symptoms of groupthink
Avoid its consequences by making clear to every member that it is creative agreement, not solidarity and cohesiveness, that is most important.

(6) When appropriate, use other decision-making methods
Alternative methods such as voting and delegating can be useful as long as fundamental disagreement is not 'smoothed over' prematurely.

REVIEW QUESTIONS

1. Think back about the meetings you were in over the last few weeks.

- Try to recall three situations where you feel the outcome could be dramatically improved, using the 'key points for negotiating within groups' listed in this book.
- Considering the 'common pitfalls in group meetings' listed in this chapter, how might you influence a future meeting to be more effective?

2. Think of a recent negotiation where you feel you communicated with less impact than you would like. Using the twelve tips for making your communication more effective, how might you make more impact next time?
3. Think about an opportunity in the near future where you could 'try out' different techniques for creative problem solving. How will you encourage other people to try them too?
4. Identify a situation at work or at home where reaching a consensus decision will be very important to the well-being of the group. Using the suggestions made by Jones and Pfeiffer, plan how you might encourage the group to pursue this approach.

CASE STUDY: MAWDESLEY ELECTRONICS COMPANY

Introduction
This case is based on a scenario developed by Price Waterhouse. It demonstrates how the structure of the situation influences the type of

negotiation climate that exists within a group of managers, and how it sets the basic conditions for achieving a joint solution. After reading the case, ask yourself the following questions:

1. What were the major difficulties for Charles in managing the meeting?
2. What pitfalls did the board members fall into?
3. What happened to ideas during the discussions?
4. How could the meeting have been conducted more effectively?

Background
Deeply disturbed by the failure of Global Enterprises, a highly respected rival company, to fight off the hostile bid of a predatory conglomerate, **Charles Green**, Chairman of Mawdesley Electronics Company (MEC), decides on an immediate meeting of the Board to review his own company's vulnerability if faced with a similar threat. It proves to be a most timely meeting with some startling revelations for the Chairman himself and for many members of his Board. Not least of which is that the value of human resources is often as critical as the cost of 'nuts and bolts'.

The Board
Charles Green rose slowly to his feet and looked around the boardroom table.

Directly to his right, is Managing Director **Peter Doyle** with whom he had founded the company some 12 years ago. Previously, Peter had worked for a major computer manufacturer. After having become increasingly frustrated with the bureaucracy of this organization, he decided to join MEC. Peter is much respected in the company. He has a reputation for never raising his voice. He hates confrontation.

Peter is currently leading the company's entry into Europe. Supposedly!

Next to him is the Financial Director, **Frank Edwards**, who joined MEC shortly after they moved the company to its current location near Southampton. He is an economics graduate from Edinburgh University and is openly contemptuous of anyone who does not think in figures. He has been a strong influence in the company's success. A hard worker, he has high standards and expects no less of his colleagues.

Beside him is **Stephen Bennett**, the Sales Director. Unquestionably a 'weighty' member of the Board, Stephen was bitterly resentful of not becoming the Marketing Director when his own organization, Office Extra, was taken over by Mawdesley last year. He had built the company from scratch but felt increasingly out of his depth in the highly competitive field of office equipment. He is very protective of 'his salesmen'.

Opposite Stephen, sits **Marie Hurley**, the Marketing Director. Although she has been with the company some time, Marie is a recent appointment to the Board. She has to deal with constant references to 'the female perspective' by her colleagues, but has proven her ability by increasing the market for the company's products consistently over the past three years despite fierce competition in a recessionary period.

Next to Marie is the irascible **Michael James**, the Production Director. Never happier than when on the shop floor where most Board members feel he spends far too much of his time.

Next to Michael, and in complete contrast, is the young and brilliant engineer **Richard Walker**, the head of Research and Development, frequently at loggerheads with Stephen and affectionately known as Maverick. He has been with Mawdesley since the early days and has acquired a reputation for flashes of genius but a short fuse.

Last, at the end of the table, is **Simon Jones**, the head of Personnel. Simon is the youngest member of the management team. Recruited from outside he has a constant battle to get the others to recognize the importance of personnel issues. People are our most valuable and expensive resource he keeps saying – others would say *ad nauseam*.

The Meeting
The meeting was called to order and Charles Green began to speak.

'You've all seen the take-over news. If Global Enterprises can fall, then we could be next. This has prompted me to bring this strategy review meeting forward six weeks. I do apologize if this has inconvenienced anyone.'

He moved swiftly on, like an Army Officer asking for any complaints but expecting none.

'Our objective today is simple' said Charles. 'We must review and develop further our Critical Success Factors.'

He turned to Peter Doyle. 'I'll now ask our Managing Director to outline the agenda. Peter.'

'Thank you, Charles.' Peter paused for effect. 'You will recall that in early discussions we had identified the five major areas we might examine to help us reach our objectives.

'The first is *"internationalization"*, and naturally I will lead on that.'

'The second subject will be *"gaining competitive advantage"*. And as this, perhaps, ought to be marketing-led, I'll ask you, Marie, to explain.'

'Excuse me, Peter, but wouldn't an input from Richard on R&D's new products be relevant here?' Marie enquired.

Peter resented Marie's response, and smiled condescendingly in her direction and said 'Of course, dear. Forgive my oversight.'. He knew the one thing she hated was being called 'dear'.

He continued 'We'll then move on to *"Information Technology – Value for Money"'* and laughing, added 'and as Frank is the only one who understands it, I'll ask him to take the reins.'

Peter bit his tongue as he wrongly made light of a touchy subject. He glanced over at Charles who hadn't missed the gaffe. He moved hurriedly on.

'Fourth on the agenda is "*Manufacturing Costs*", where I expect Michael and Richard to do a double act.'

'When we come to the delicate subject of "*Management Succession*" I suspect Charles will want to lead with Simon, our new Personnel Director, assisting.'

Simon Jones looked up at the M.D. and smiled. 'I think you'll find, Peter, I have a contribution to make not only on management succession, but on most of the earlier subjects, too.'

It wasn't meant to sound threatening.

If the discussion on internationalization was to set the pattern for the day, they were in for a long and bumpy ride.

As Simon feared, Peter's idea of entering Europe was making half-a-dozen junkets to Paris with Stephen in tow. And it was very noticeable that Marie had *never* been invited along.

Planning and organization had so far been confined to the setting up of an agency network. An arrangement cynically referred to by Frank as '*our comedie Française*'.

As far as staffing up for the internationalization programme was concerned, a young marketing graduate had been asked to go to Paris, had refused the salary offered, and then been encouraged to resign.

There were some genuine excuses for this sad situation. For instance, for the last nine months, Peter, Stephen and Marie had all been involved in preparing for a major exhibition at Birmingham NEC – a vitally important event for the company's profile in UK markets. However, this did not excuse the fact that Richard had been allocated no additional people or funds for R&D to produce new items aimed specifically at the European market.

At this point, Simon asked if any thought had been given to adjusting the company's basic culture to assist the move towards internationalization.

'Good point' said Marie, aiming her next comment at Stephen. 'How many of our current sales force speak a foreign language?'. Simon suspected she already knew the answer.

'Wearing a beret and riding an onion-seller's bicycle is hardly likely to increase our sales in France' retorted Stephen.

'That's not what . . .' Marie started, when Simon decided it was time to intervene. First, by posing a few questions.

'Have we really thought about how best to market and sell in Europe? What sort of organization do we need and what kind of people to run it? Where do we find them? Can we fund the costs of recruitment, compensation and training?'

'What is the cost of getting into Europe likely to be?' asked Frank, nervously.

'A lot less than the cost of *not* getting in' replied Stephen.

'What's *your* answer, then?' Peter challenged Simon.

'Well in fairness, I think you and the team here have enough to do to maintain and improve our UK position.'

They liked that. But would Peter buy his next proposition?

'I believe it's time we appointed a new key person to head up our internationalization programme.' He continued swiftly. 'We may already have someone suitable internally. We may have to recruit. We'll almost certainly need outside advice – if we're really serious about Europe.'

Simon looked across at Charles. His expression showed that he was.

Peter's expression was far less charitable.

Some six months ago, MEC had made a conscious decision to move from its 'Low Delivered Cost' policy in favour of a 'High Perceived Value' route. So far, it had proved less than a raging success.

'I agreed to change my marketing strategy only if certain conditions could be met' protested Marie, looking pointedly in Charles's direction.

'Unfortunately, we've failed to raise our product quality, been slow to improve our customer service, and although we've mounted a bullish advertising and PR campaign, we're still stuck with a down-market image.'

On the sales side, Stephen told a similar tale of woe. 'I promised my sales force innovative products to crack the new markets. So far we've had one. And that gave us so many warranty problems that we've lost orders for our traditional ranges.'

Richard responded, angrily 'It was an excellent product badly manu-factured'. At which, Frank jumped in. 'Meanwhile, we've increased our unit cost by eight per cent by agreeing an across-the-board quality control bonus. Madness!'

Michael, for once, was quite restrained in his reply. 'Frank. We're supposed to be discussing manufacturing costs later. Then I'll have something to say about your snide remarks and your penny-pinching attitude to production people.'

Simon tried to cool the situation.

'You're right, Michael. You shouldn't put profit before people. But it's not a crime to make people profitable.' He continued 'But do our people know about our change to an HPV policy? What have we done about internal communication to change employee attitudes on quality and customer care?' He looked at Marie. 'Have we retrained the workforce to produce high quality instead of high output? Have we emphasized the need for fewer errors and the importance of getting things "right first time"? Have we got the right people in supervisory roles? And have we trained them in how to carry them out?'

These were the questions – but they had to find the answers if MEC were ever going to gain a competitive edge.

Simon's heart sank when the discussion turned to Information Tech-nology – Value for Money.

It was immediately obvious that although the subject was on the agenda, most Board members just didn't understand it. Simon made a mental note 'First, educate the Board'.

This total lack of expertise left the ball, quite wrongly, in Frank's court – simply because the one area the Board could identify with computers was the accounting function. But Simon knew the system MEC had installed was capable of much more than that. He doubted whether Frank did. For instance, why did he continue to use a bureau processing service to handle wages and salaries when he had sufficient machine capacity to run a simple pay-roll package in-house? Why didn't he have a software module to aid him with his Corporate Tax accounting? And why had it taken Simon's own arrival at the company for them to consider computerizing the personnel function?

The discussion deteriorated to a few mutterings about deadlines being missed, customers complaining about late invoicing and incorrect statements. Michael James asked some unintelligible questions about CAD/ CAM, but nobody seemed to know or much care whether the huge investment in technology was paying off.

It was clear that if IT were to play any part in the organization, management and production at MEC, there would have to be a dramatic change in attitude.

Simon began to make copious notes: Educate to heighten awareness of IT. What can IT do *specifically* for MEC? Can our current people work with IT? Should we introduce aptitude testing or perhaps establish assessment centres? Find suitable training courses?

'All very well' thought Simon. 'But who, apart from himself, was going to implement and oversee this programme?' He made a larger note: another area for a new key appointment?

The discussion on Manufacturing Costs was to prove perhaps the most convoluted of all the day's subjects. Frank Edwards was adamant the solution of the company's recent cost problems was to scrap the quality bonus payments introduced when PLC changed to HPV production.

'We should have held out for a single-union agreement at the time, and insisted on a flexibility deal then' said Frank.

'And then use a Japanese style system making every man his own quality controller, I suppose' laughed Michael.

Even Marie found it amusing. 'If we do ever try it, will someone give me time to arrange a decent press release explaining the strike to our customers!?'

'Anyway' continued Michael to Frank 'why do you always blame labour costs for our problems? If we'd put some investment into new plants instead of R&D's highfalutin ideas, the modern machinery would have given us automatic quality control. And we would have been using fewer operatives and inspectors.'.

Richard protested at the suggestion his R&D budget was high. 'In real terms, R&D expenditure hasn't risen for two years. If it had, we might by now have been able to "design-in" quality at the outset.'

Marie put forward another view. 'I've always said we could reduce our costs by rationalizing our locations in relation to our markets.'

Suddenly Peter shot to his feet. He was flushed and red angry. 'For Heaven's sake. Please. Can anyone tell me where our true costs are?'

Michael retorted 'You might find the answer from the blokes on the shop floor. If any of you know where it is!'

'Good idea, Michael, if we can get your people to help us' said Simon. 'We do need to ask some pertinent questions. Do we know that we're paying the right rates to the right people? Are we getting value for money from the bonus system? Do people really understand what they have to do – or is it that the supervisors and managers don't understand what the system is meant to achieve? Are we in fact paying for performance or not?'

Before Michael could intervene, Simon turned to Frank. 'But that only touches on labour costs, Frank. What about our overall costing system? When did we last examine it? How good is it in our new quality production environment? Can it really identify cost areas? And quite frankly, have we got the right people to run, let alone test the system? Which in some ways throws us back to our last subject. Will we ever know our true manufacturing costs if we don't use the correct Information Technology?'

Simon again wrote 'PEOPLE'? on his pad.

To give him his due, Charles pulled a few punches in tackling the delicate area of Management Succession – a subject some cynics have labelled 'Outplacement and Early Retirement Plans'.

Charles first talked about the unexpected take-over success which had prompted this strategy review meeting. He pointed out that the victorious conglomerate claimed its success had been gained because of its promise to 'shake-up the management'.

'Let me read you one criticism from the bid document' said Charles. 'The company has an ageing Board, and its Senior Management is predominantly in the 40s and 50s age group. Both the Board and the management are mainly home-grown, in-bred and too engineering-biased. There is no sign of new blood.'

'Sounds familiar?' asked Charles, continuing

'We plan to revitalize what is fundamentally an excellent company by putting the right people in the right place.'

'Well' said Charles 'We intend to put that aspect right for ourselves. I'll let Simon Jones, our new Personnel Director explain.'

Simon, of course, had no intention of going into great detail in such an open meeting. But he outlined the major areas of concern, indirectly inviting each relevant Board member to assist him in his task. He emphasized that he would need help to avoid the 'people' mistakes Charles has just highlighted. 'We must first establish what the company expects of its people – including this Board. We must then take stock of our managerial talent; identify the key players and the gaps which we need to fill. And we must develop a human resources strategy – based on our business plan – which helps us fill those gaps. There is also a need to implement a manpower plan and a formal succession plan – but this must not stop individuals who are on the "fast track".'

Some of the Board remained passive. Others nodded approval. Simon continued. 'We must build on skills, encourage ambition and clearly define management roles. And we must spell out the rewards we offer for performance and success. Finally, we must analyse our training methods and our management development programmes to encourage more effective performance' he paused. Then without looking up. 'From the Board down.'

The silence seemed eternal, until Marie said 'It sounds exciting, Simon. Could we get together to discuss what this means for marketing?'.

He got the impression that a request from Ms Hurley always sounded more like a command.

Naturally, the meeting had caused a certain amount of unease. The members of the Board seemed shaken by much of what had been said. Charles relaxed the atmosphere by calling the meeting to a halt. 'Well, we've all got a lot to think about. I'd like to meet again early next week to agree on what we're going to do.'

'It's essential, Charles' Simon replied. 'It seems to me that most of our problems revolve around the people dimensions; how we are structured and organized; how we identify and develop talent; how we motivate and reward our people – from the Board down; how we help our people achieve the goals which we *should* be setting them.'

4

Negotiating between groups

He who fights with monsters might take care lest he thereby
become a monster. (G. W. Nietzsche, 1844–1900)

Negotiations between groups such as countries, organizations or
departments follow the same general format that you find in
negotiations between two or more individuals. In terms of how each
side should prepare, open, discuss and close the negotiations, all
the same considerations apply in an inter-group situation as between individuals. However, negotiations between groups are more
likely to fail as one or more parties typically see themselves as
having the power to alter substantially the other parties' aspirations
and goals.

How can conflicts between groups be resolved successfully through negotiating?
And related to this, how can we get win–win settlements from
inter-group negotiation without suffering the destructive side effects
of inter-group competition and conflict escalation? This chapter
focuses on three aspects of successful inter-group negotiations:

1. Effective teamwork.

2. Forming and maintaining coalitions.

3. Devising integrative solutions.

Teamwork

The hammers must be swung in cadence, when more than one is
hammering the iron. (Giordano Bruno, 1548–1600)

Many of the most important negotiations between organizations or
groups are handled by teams that represent the larger collectives.
For instance, in international negotiations, which usually involve
many complicated issues, it is often expedient for top diplomats and
their aides to negotiate the underlying principles or a framework of
the overall agreement. Smaller, specialized committees, consisting of
lower-ranking diplomats on both sides, then negotiate the finer
details (Pruitt and Carnevale, 1993).

What is needed for effective teamwork?
To be effective, negotiating teams need to co-ordinate the activities
of the individuals participating in the discussion. Each team is
supposed to work as an integrated unit and function with a single
purpose in pursuit of one set of priorities. Members of a negotiation
team may disagree on the substance of the negotiation (what offers
to make) and on the best style to adopt (how to negotiate, when to
make an offer, whether threats should be used and so on). For
instance, while some members may prefer to avoid the consequences of conflict and non-settlement, seeing them as destructive;
other members of the team might prefer to see bargaining as 'a raw
contest of will and power' rather than to compromise or agree with
the proposals of the other side. Differences like these, between team
members, need to be resolved as a prerequisite to effective negotiation with the other group. Unless some means exist for bringing
together and co-ordinating both goals and positions within the
team, there will be serious communication problems at the negotiating table.

What roles are needed?
To ensure effective teamwork, it is advisable to allocate certain roles
to members of the negotiating team. These roles include a 'Spokesperson', a 'Back-up' and one or more 'Observers'.

The **spokesperson** will normally be the most experienced negotiator in the team. His or her role is to communicate with the other
party.

The **back-up** acts as the spokesperson's assistant. This role is

Key points for managing your negotiating team

Guidelines:

- Reflect on specific strengths and weaknesses of the team. Be aware of each member's abilities and how to bring these into play to complement the abilities of others on the team.

- Structure team discussion and debate to deepen understanding of objectives.

- Draw a clear line of authority. Agree in advance who will be the spokesperson, who is the back-up and who observes. Some people like to have a 'hard person' and a 'soft person' in their team. However, this needs careful planning and co-ordinating in order to avoid contradictory statements.

- Team members should support each other verbally and non-verbally during the negotiation. However, the spokesperson needs to be the one who controls the negotiating process and decides when another team member should speak.

- There is usually no need to keep the same team throughout the negotiations. As the discussions develop, the need for specific forms of expertise may change. For example, it may be useful to have legal experts present for the opening stage, leave their seat vacant during the bargaining stage, and bring them back for the closing.

- Plan how to communicate within your team during the negotiations.

- Review your teamwork regularly and develop improvements to make the team more effective.

- Admit when you and your team fall short of the ideal.

- Learn from mistakes as well as successes.

Pitfalls to avoid:

- Autocratic team leadership. Trying to do everything yourself before and during the negotiation.

- Blaming someone else for every mistake and difficulty.

- Assuming everybody knows how to communicate within the team.

- Worrying only about what is being discussed during the negotiation, not how the discussion is progressing.

- Failing to establish a united front on goals and strategy before going into negotiation sessions.

predominantly to (i) buy time for the spokesperson when it might be difficult to make a response, (ii) call the adjournments and (iii) summarize the contents of the meeting. Experience shows that it is extremely difficult for a single person to talk, think, listen and understand in negotiation. The back-up role is to help the spokesperson cope with this problem.

The role of the **observer(s)** is to (i) watch the other team carefully, looking for verbal or non-verbal signals which might reveal their thinking, (ii) take notes, (iii) report to the spokesperson during or after the meeting, and (iv) provide specialist advice during adjournments.

Who else may be involved?

Experts and specialists can sometimes be invited to participate in the negotiations. However, adding people solely to match the other party's team size is not very sensible. An effective team does not have to be of the same size as the other side's. As Gavin Kennedy (1993) says 'there is no safety in numbers, only expense'.

Forming coalitions

All for one, one for all. (Les Trois Mousquetiers, Alexander Dumas, 1824–1895)

Multilateral negotiation, involving more than two individuals or organizations, is a phenomenon that is becoming increasingly common, and therefore important, as network companies grow in prominence and more and more actors become involved in negotiating. The presence of many parties at the bargaining table greatly complicates the process. In such cases, coalitions may be formed between two or more parties. Some coalitions may hold for the entire negotiation, but often alliances shift with various issues.

How effective are coalitions in negotiation?

The evidence is mixed. On the one hand, one finds that coalitions:

- Are often far more effective in achieving negotiated settlements than one-to-one talks. When many parties are involved, like in the GATT talks, it usually requires much more time to forge an agreement between individual parties than between coalitions.

- Can help decisions and solutions be accepted and implemented by individual members.

On the other hand, research suggests that coalitions:

- Often end up with less than desirable agreements because of the need to achieve a consensus.
- Often come up with a solution that is more mediocre than its best individual member would arrive at – but one which is usually more acceptable and more workable.
- Can be quite resistant to change.
- Have built-in restrictions on innovation and creativity.
- At times, have individual members who will protect their own provincial interests at the expense of the overall good.

Clearly, forming coalitions is a two-edged sword. So it is necessary to know what kind of groups you are dealing with, how each group interacts and responds to other groups and what strategies you will use in coping with the key issues and problems that inhibit effective negotiating.

What are the problems associated with maintaining a coalition?

Once formed, maintaining a coalition is always a fine balancing act. Very often problems arise because:

- One member dominates the coalition.
- Jealousy emerges between members.
- There are conflicting goals, agendas or strategies.
- The coalition becomes too formal.
- There are too many meetings.
- The work assigned to one of the members does not get done.

How can you make a coalition work?

All the above problems can be overcome. Here are just a few suggestions for making your coalitions work (Vanover, 1980):

- Clearly define issues and strategy. Disarray in a coalition is usually a result of a dispute about the bargaining objectives, one group preferring a soft approach (the doves), the other preferring a tougher line (the hawks).

- Divide up tasks within the coalition. Determine resources, budget, and meet those needs.
- Select leadership from within the alliance. Someone must call the shots. Choose someone with a commitment to the alliance and time to devote to it.
- Develop an internal communication programme. Remember to keep all coalition partners informed and involved, whether through meetings, newsletters, memos or telephone calls.

Twenty tips for making a coalition work

According to Eddy Fraser, president of Fraser/Associates in Washington D.C., there are 20 rules for participating in an effective coalition (quoted in Lewicki and Litterer, 1985). They are:

1. Clearly define own issues and strategy.
2. Determine a timetable and needs.
3. Identify both potential allies and opposition.
4. Build your constituency and recruit allies.
5. Select leadership from within the coalition.
6. Devise a clear plan of action for the coalition.
7. Determine necessary resources and meet those requirements.
8. Divide up tasks within the coalition.
9. Establish a working task force or executive committee.
10. Keep coalition members informed and involved.
11. Establish a communication plan.
12. Build supportive case materials.
13. Develop an internal communication programme with each association involving its members.
14. Enlist experts to support the coalition case.
15. Explain the issue in terms of economic impact when possible.
16. Utilize all pertinent media for greatest impact.
17. Remember to keep all coalition constituents informed and involved.
18. If it is a legislative issue, review the government strategy on a regular basis.
19. Determine if the coalition leadership is serving as a catalyst for communication.
20. Prove the results and communicate them to the member constituencies.

Building integrative agreements

How can I get from here to there by a route that doesn't seem possible? (S. Wozniak, co-founder Apple Computers, 1988)

An integrative agreement is one that reconciles the parties' interests. Integrative agreements produce solutions that are more satisfying to the negotiators than compromises, tossing a coin and other mechanical types of agreements. Remember the story of two sisters who were quarrelling over an orange. A compromise agreement was reached by splitting the fruit in half, then the first sister squeezed her half for juice while the other sister used the peel in a cake. Clearly, they would both have benefited more from the integrative solution of giving the first sister all the juice and the second all the peel, but, looking for a compromise, they never considered it.

How can you achieve integrative agreements?
Integrative agreements are sometimes based on known alternatives, but more often than not they involve the development of novel ones. Therefore, they require a considerable amount of creativity and imagination. It is also true that not all negotiations have the potential for such solutions. For example, there is little opportunity for developing integrative solutions when both parties want all the available resources, or when they are simply out to do as well as they can for themselves, without regard for how well or poorly the other party is doing.

What are the routes for moving from opposing demands to a solution that reconciles the two parties' interests?
Pruitt and Rubin (1986) have identified five such routes, leading to five types of integrative agreements. Their model is illustrated by an example concerning a husband and wife who are trying to decide where to go on holiday. The husband prefers to go to the mountains, the wife to the seaside. They have considered the compromise of spending one week in each location but are hoping for something better. What approach should they take?

(1) They can 'expand the pie'
Some integrative agreements are built by increasing the available resources so that both sides can get what they want. For example our couple might solve the problem by persuading their employers

to give them additional days of vacation so that they can spend some time in the mountains and some time at the seashore.

(2)   They can use 'log-rolling'

A second way to build integrative agreements is to exchange concessions on different issues, with each party yielding on issues that are of low priority for themselves and of high priority to the other party. For example, if, as well as disagreeing where to go on holiday, the wife in our example prefers a first-class hotel and the husband wants to go camping (i.e. accommodation is most important to the wife and location is most important to the husband) they can reach a fairly integrative agreement by going to a first-class hotel in the mountains.

(3)   They can make trade-offs

Such trade-offs are sometimes achieved through '*non-specific compensation*'. Here one party gets what it wants and the other is repaid on some unrelated issue. For example, the wife might agree to go to the mountains if her husband agrees that some of the money can be spent on buying her a new car.

(4)   They can reach agreement through 'cost cutting'

This happens when somebody (one of the negotiators or a third party) examines the concerns that underlie the positions taken by one or more of the parties and looks for a way to achieve these concerns. Sometimes only one party's concerns need to be examined, because that party will accept the other's demands if these concerns are met. For instance suppose that the husband in our example dislikes the beach because of the noise and crowd. He might be quite willing to go there on holiday if his costs are cut by finding a hotel where he can enjoy his privacy while his wife goes out among the crowds.

(5)   They can look for 'bridging' solutions

Such solutions are devised by an analysis of both parties' underlying concerns. As in the earlier example of the two sisters arguing over an orange, our couple may invent a novel solution that satisfies the most important interests of both parties. For example, suppose that the husband is mainly interested in fishing and the wife wants mainly to swim, these interests might be bridged by finding a seaside resort with a harbour that is close to a beach.

These various methods of building integrative agreements can serve as a check-list for trying to find creative ways to resolve any conflict. Associated with each method there is a set of 'refocusing' questions, which are useful for identifying the win–win options (Pruitt and Rubin, 1986). These questions are listed in the box below.

Key questions for devising integrative solutions

For expanding the pie:

- How can both parties get what they are demanding?
- Is there a resource shortage?
- How can the critical resource be expanded?

For log-rolling:

- What issues are of higher and lower priority to myself?
- What issues are of higher and lower priority to the other party?
- Are some of my high-priority issues, low priority to the other party and vice versa?
- Are several issues bundled together (for either party) which can be separated?

For non-specific compensation:

- What are the other party's goals and values?
- What can I do to satisfy them?

For cost-cutting:

- What risks and costs does my proposal pose for the other party?
- How can these risks and costs be mitigated?

For bridging:

- What underlying concerns are served by the other party's proposal?
- What underlying concerns are served by my proposal?
- What are the two parties' priorities among these underlying concerns?
- How can both parties' high priority concerns be served?

Which approach works best?

The questions listed for expanding the pie show that this kind of solution can be achieved with no knowledge about the other party except his/her demands. This is also sometimes true of log-rolling solutions, where only the first question, about your own priorities, is absolutely essential. If the first question is answered, log-rolling solutions can sometimes be achieved by means of systematic concession making. This involves starting with high goals and proposing all the combinations of options you can think of that serve these goals.

If none of these combinations is accepted by the other party, you relax or drop your lower priority goals and again propose all possible combinations, continuing this cycle until the other party accepts a proposal. Although this is a possible route to log-rolling solutions, these solutions can usually be achieved more efficiently if the other party's priorities are also known.

The other routes to integrative agreements require some knowledge about the other party, and these requirements become greater as you go down the list. Bridging, at the bottom of the list, requires detailed and intimate information about the other party's underlying concerns and the priorities among these concerns. This implies that it will be harder to reach agreement in settings that require solutions that are further down this list.

Achieving integrative agreements through 'principled negotiation'
One of the best known approaches to negotiation was proposed by Fisher and Ury (1981) in their best-seller *Getting To Yes*.

According to these authors, the following strategies have been shown to produce integrative solutions.

(1)   Establish superordinate goals
To foster a climate of collaboration, the parties need to focus on what they have in common. This step is initiated by the general question 'What common goals provide a context for our discussions?'. In a business context, this can be a shared concern for increased productivity, better quality, improved morale and so on.

(2)   Separate the people from the problem
Negotiations are more likely to produce integrative results if the parties depersonalize the issues. The other party is viewed as the advocate of a different point of view, rather than as an enemy. Principled negotiators do not use personal attacks to humiliate the other party.

(3)   Focus on interests, not positions
Positions are the demands and offers that negotiators make. Interests are the underlying reasons for making them. Agreements are built on the basis of reconciling the interests of the parties, rather than by making extreme opening demands and then looking for compromises.

(4) Invent options for mutual gain
By focusing on interests, principled negotiators search for solutions that satisfy 100 per cent of the needs of the negotiators. This requires creativity, openness about real interests, and above all, patience.

(5) Use objective criteria
Integrative solutions do not reflect the balance of power, or the willingness to concede, among the parties. They are based on what is fair and feasible under the circumstances. This requires a shift in the attitudes and behaviours of the parties from 'getting what I can' to 'deciding what is fair and reasonable for both parties'.

It is obvious that this approach is not equally attractive to all individuals. Some people tend to prefer a more confrontational strategy. In addition, principled bargaining is unlikely to work when one or more parties is inexperienced or when there is a lack of openness and trust between the negotiators. However, as a general-purpose strategy, principled negotiation is much better than the traditional 'positional bargaining' approach for generating integrative agreements.

REVIEW QUESTIONS

1. Think of a recent situation at work (or elsewhere) where you were part of a team in a multiparty negotiation and answer the following questions:

    (a) Which roles did individuals within the team adopt and how effective were they?

    (b) Using the guidelines in this section, what steps could be taken to improve your teamwork?

    (c) Which pitfalls (if any) did you fall into and how might they be avoided in future?

2. Think of a situation where you operate in a coalition. How well does it work? Using Fraser's 20 tips for making a coalition work, what steps could you take to make it more effective?

3. Think of a past negotiation where you have found it difficult (or failed) to reach agreement. With the great benefit of hindsight how might you have used the following routes to reach an integrative agreement?

    (a) expanding the pie

    (b) log-rolling

(c) trade-off

(d) non-specific compensation

(e) cost-cutting

(f) bridging

4. Think of a negotiation you will be party to in the near future. Using the description of the basic strategies involved in principled negotiation, how might this approach help you reach an integrative agreement?

5. What conditions are needed to make integrative agreements possible?

CASE STUDY: INTERNATIONAL COMPUTER SYSTEMS

Introduction

This case is based on a role-playing exercise called 'Universal Computer Company' by Lewicki and Litterer (1985). After reading the background information, try to answer the following questions:

1. How do you propose that the following problems and issues be resolved by the two groups of representatives?

   • Expense of repairing all faulty modules sold.

   • Expense of inspecting and repairing or replacing faulty computers in stock.

   • Expense and replacement of faulty chips in stock.

   • Expense of identifying and eliminating the cause of the quality problem.

2. What opportunities can you see in this case for achieving an integrative solution through the following methods:

   • expanding the pie
   • log-rolling
   • non-specific compensation
   • bridging
   • cost-cutting

3. Which solution is likely to work best? What does this say about how to deal with financial issues in inter-group negotiations?

Background information

International Computer Systems (ICS) is one of the world's largest manufacturers of mini, micro and mainframe computers. It was founded about 30 years ago by several young computer wizards from Cal Tech. Today the organization, while vertically integrated, is extremely decentralized. There are separate divisions assembling mainframe, mini and micro computers. Each division is run as a profit centre. Divisions are managed by a division vice-president who reports to the president of the corporation.

Three years ago, ICS began manufacturing a new model personal computer, called 'MERLIN', and it was a major success. The assembly plan was running at capacity and having trouble keeping up with sales. Furthermore, the division vice-president was putting considerable pressure on the assembly plant manager to increase capacity in order to take advantage of the favourable press MERLIN was getting.

This was not the least of the plant manager's problems. Four weeks into production, John Kendall, MERLIN's product manager, started getting calls from distributors who, in turn, were getting calls from unhappy customers complaining that they could not get printers, which were supposed to be compatible with the new model computer, to work. In fact, a quality control check of the 200 MERLINs assembled each day showed 34 per cent of computers having printer difficulties. As a result, the engineers responsible for the MERLIN assembly process worked round-the-clock to identify the cause of this problem. They told Kendall that they believed the problem could be traced to five ROM (read only memory) chips. These chips contained the basic input/output systems software and were located on one of MERLINs printed circuit boards.

ICS purchased its integrated circuits, or 'chips', including the five ROM chips in question, from a small manufacturing company called Universal Data Devices (UDD). The chips supplied by UDD were soldered onto boards in one of ICS's computer assembly plants. The plant engineers ruled out a problem with the board itself. The boards were passing incoming quality control at a rate higher than specified and none of the tests of assembled boards indicated a board problem.

In contrast, the ICS engineers working on the MERLIN, had done a random check of each type of ROM chip in stock and found that, overall, 5 per cent of the UDD chips used in MERLIN were defective. This was significantly higher than the 5 per thousand default rate guaranteed by Universal.

It was conceivable that ICS could use an alternative supplier and purchase the five ROM chips for MERLIN elsewhere. Kendall did not know, however, how quickly these chips could be supplied by others. One of his purchasing managers checked around for another supplier for the five ROM chips supplied by Universal. He found that market prices were between 4 and 5 per cent cheaper than ICS had been paying to UDD for integrated circuits. However, no single supplier could provide all five chips. Furthermore, two alternative suppliers reported that they were also having quality control problems with the types of ROM chips used in MERLIN. A third potential supplier had a backlog of orders and the earliest delivery date he could quote was in 15 days.

Subsequently, Kendall called Hugh Braddick, vice-president of Universal Data Devices, and told him that 5 per cent of their ROM chips were found to be defective. He asked Braddick if UDD was operating on a quality control standard different from the guaranteed 5 per thousand. Braddick said his company was not having problems with other customers buying the same types of ROM chips. He questioned the analysis done by ICS engineers but said he and his colleagues would be prepared to discuss the quality control problems with representatives from ICS. Kendall agreed to arrange a meeting and the two sides agreed to meet at the ICS headquarters.

It was of course important to ICS to make every effort to discuss the problem with UDD in as friendly a manner as possible. However, there was no doubt that there was a fair amount of feeling amongst ICS managers that UDD was responsible for the quality problems. It looked as if they wanted UDD managers to take all the blame and pay for the consequences.

During the meeting, the ICS representatives argued UDD had a deliver-to-stock arrangement with computer manufacturers such as ICS. This meant the company guaranteed a 5 per thousand quality rate for every type of chip supplied and customers should not have to test incoming devices. According to Kendall, ICS engineers did not know what percentage of chips UDD was sample-testing. However, they felt greater specification of the quality control (QC) standard might reduce the number of faulty chips supplied. Their view was that Universal ought to test 100 per cent of the ROM chips made for MERLIN.

Kendall said ICS needed only to do a random check of ten per cent of the incoming ROM chips in order to monitor the deliver-to-stock agreement. However, that test was going to cost a lot of money and it required personnel which his company did not have but which UDD almost certainly did have available. He therefore suggested UDD might send a small team of QC engineers to carry out the quality control checks of all incoming chips in the assembly plant, at their expense.

The UDD representatives replied that their engineers had done their best to enforce a 5 per thousand default standard on every type of chip that went out of the integrated circuits factory. However, it was extremely difficult to apply that standard to the five ROM chips used in MERLIN. As Braddick put it:

> ROM chips are in an almost constant state of flux as new products are constantly coming on the market and integrated circuit technology develops and changes rapidly. All this change plays havoc with quality control and inspection.

According to Braddick, the five ROM chips that were made for MERLIN were using new technology which made them extremely sensitive to problems with static electricity. 'Static' he said 'can make the chips short out and malfunction'. In fact, two weeks earlier, another client of UDD had been having similar problems with some of the ROM chips. The company sent over a team to try to ferret out the problem. The team found that the chips were picking up some static electricity in transit and further static in processing. The client switched to the anti-static trays for shipping and the customer put in anti-static floors. This customer's problems then seemed to be resolved. Braddick suggested ICS probably had the same problem with static that everyone else had been discovering with this new generation of ROM chips.

That same customer had a front-end quality inspection procedure for these chips and was only finding a 1 per cent defect rate. This customer was so satisfied that he was negotiating to buy a larger volume of ROM chips. He said he could use about 60 per cent of the volume UDD was now selling to the ICS computer assembly plant.

If relations with ICS got very bad, it was conceivable that UDD could decide to go with the alternative customer and let ICS purchase its ROM chips for MERLIN elsewhere. UDD did not know, however, how quickly the resulting 40 per cent excess capacity could be marketed, especially since the prices of its ROM chips were between 4 and 5 per cent higher than those of competitors.

Besides, if ICS decided to go to another supplier for the five chips in question, UDD might have to cut back its work force. Also, word was likely to get around that the firm was looking for customers for chips that ICS was trying to acquire elsewhere. This would not help UDD's market reputation.

UDD managers certainly did not want to take any responsibility for the defective MERLINs. After all, they said, the computers passed the PC plant's final inspection. If they did take responsibility, ICS could blame them for everything that might go wrong in the future. Moreover, their engineers were convinced that a large part of the problem was static generated in shipping, warehousing and handling the chips, none of which was UDD's responsibility. Nonetheless, if ICS pushed very hard they might consider paying a portion of the cost of repairing the defective MERLINs.

At the time, UDD produced approximately 500 different types of chips for computers. It sample-tested about 20 per cent of these chips, including the five used in MERLIN. Greater specification of the quality control standard would reduce the production plant's flexibility. The managers certainly did not want to test 100 per cent of ROM chips made in their plant.

As for the assembled MERLINs, 48 000 had been sold. At a 30 per cent default rate, that could be 14 400 faulty computers which must be identified and repaired. Probably the most thorough repair procedure would be to have the dealers check the board with the five ROM chips which seem to cause the problem. These chips cost between £10 and £50 each. This meant the total cost of replacement could be as high as £1.9 million (£130 per faulty computer) without considering the premium needed to pay ICS dealers for testing and repairing the faulty computers.

Kendall suggested this might cost £150 per computer. Thus, the total cost of repair could be £4.6 million assuming that not too many customers would bring in computers for testing that turned out to have no chip problems.

One potential solution to the problem was to ship the entire ROM stock back to UDD and get a new delivery which checked out at 5 per thousand. The problem with this approach was that the MERLIN assembly line was already shut down. Besides, UDD did not have sufficient ROM chips available to replace the existing stock which was estimated to be about 1000 of each type of chip (or 5000 chips in all) and it did not have the staff to run quality control checks on every chip in stock. The company did, however, have the technology to do such tests and it could send to ICS, at their cost, a small team to train *their* assembly workers to do the quality control checks.

5

Negotiating among cultures

It is useful to know something about other nations' habits in
order to judge our own in a healthier fashion, and not to
imagine everything which differs from ours should be
dismissed as ridiculous or illogical, as is frequently done by
those who haven't seen anything. (Descartes, 1596–1650)

One of the biggest mistakes in any discussion of negotiation
practices is to ignore differences between cultures. What makes
someone a good negotiator in one culture may well not work in
another. As Prabhu Guptara says, different social groups have
different ideas of what is proper protocol and procedure. The
emphasis placed on preliminaries varies, and the order and spirit in
which different elements of negotiation are approached can be
radically different among cultures. For example, Japanese managers
describe effective negotiators as dedicated, able to perceive and
exploit power, able to win respect and confidence, and having
integrity, good listening skills and verbal expressiveness. American
managers only emphasize product knowledge and verbal ability,
while to the Chinese, a good negotiator must be an interesting
person, have good judgement, demonstrate product knowledge,
and intelligence.

This chapter deals with some of the major aspects of inter-cultural
negotiation by:

1. Looking at some of the key differences between (national)
   cultures and their implications for actual negotiating.

2. Offering some suggestions for negotiating successfully with people from different cultural backgrounds.

Understanding different cultures

> The first condition of understanding a foreign country is to smell it. (T.S. Eliot, 1888)

How do cultures vary?

It is difficult to do justice to this vast subject. However, to get a better understanding of the different ways of thinking, feeling and behaving in different cultures and countries, consider the findings of four academics who have been exploring the cultural differences between nations by examining the following set of questions:

1. Fons Trompenaars: What happens when a close friend is potentially in serious trouble with the law?
2. Geert Hofstede: How do different cultures define what is fair, reasonable and proper behaviour?
3. André Laurent: Should managers always have answers to subordinates' questions?
4. Michael Bond: How do attitudes to time differ between cultures?

(1) Fons Trompenaars
Fons Trompenaars, a Dutch consultant doing research on cultural differences in multinational organizations, confronted 15 000 managers from 50 different countries with the following scenario:

> You are riding in a car driven by a close friend. He hits a pedestrian. You know he was going at least 35 miles per hour in an area of the city where the maximum allowed speed is 20 miles per hour. There are no witnesses. His lawyer says that if you testify under oath that he was only driving 20 miles per hour it may save him from serious consequences.

Question 1: What right has your friend to expect you to protect him?
Answers:
(a) My friend has a definite right to expect me to testify to the lower figure.

(b)   He has some right as a friend to expect me to testify to the lower figure.

(c)   He has no right as a friend to expect me to testify to the lower figure.

Question 2: What do you think you would do in view of the obligations of a sworn witness and the obligation to your friend?
Answers:
(d)   Testify that he was going 20 miles an hour.

(e)   Not testify that he was going 20 miles an hour.

Not surprisingly the responses differed significantly among cultures.

- North Americans and most north Europeans emerged as almost totally 'universalist' in their approach to the problem, the majority of respondents choosing either (c) or (b + e). This approach is roughly 'What is good and right can be defined and always applies'.

- 70 per cent of the French and the Japanese people chose options (c) or (b + e). Over one third of the respondents chose either (a) or (d).

- In Russia, Venezuela, Indonesia and China, more than half of respondents said they would lie to the police to protect their friend, apparently reasoning 'my friend needs my help more than ever now that he is in serious trouble with the law'.

(2)   Geert Hofstede
In a landmark study of national cultures, Geert Hofstede (another Dutchman working in the field of international management and organization), analysed survey data from 116 000 employees of IBM in over fifty different countries during the period 1967–73. Hofstede's findings show that:

1.   People from different countries have very different views of what is fair, reasonable and proper behaviour.

2.   These differences can be explained to a large extent by the following four key factors.

(i) Power distance. This indicates the extent to which a society accepts and expects that power in institutions and organizations is distributed unequally. More specifically, power distance is associ-

ated with the degree of centralization of authority and the extent of autocratic leadership.

- **'High power distance'** cultures are characterized by bosses who have much more power than their subordinates, power-holders who are entitled to privileges and subordinates who consider superiors as a different kind of people. Examples of such cultures include Portugal, Greece, France and Belgium.

- **'Low power distance'** cultures are characterized by employees expecting superiors to be accessible and frequently bypassing their boss in order to get their work done. Examples are Denmark, Norway and Great Britain.

(ii) Masculinity. This is the extent to which the dominant values in society are 'male' – values such as assertiveness, the acquisition of money and goods, and not caring for others. Masculine societies also define gender roles more rigidly than do 'feminine' societies.

Hofstede's findings suggest that Scandinavian countries are the most feminine, the United States is moderately masculine and Japan and Austria are highly masculine.

(iii) Individualism. This is the opposite of collectivism and describes the extent to which individuals are integrated into groups. Where individualism is high, people expect to take care only of themselves and their immediate families and their relatives to look after them and be more loyal to them, in exchange. Members of individualistic societies also place emphasis on self-respect; members of collectivist cultures place more importance on fitting in harmoniously and face-saving.

Individualism is highest in Anglo-Saxon countries, Italy, Belgium and France; it is much lower in Spain, Greece, Portugal, Latin American countries and Japan.

(iv) Uncertainty avoidance. This factor measures the extent to which people in a society feel threatened by ambiguous situations and the extent to which they try to avoid unstructured situations by providing greater career stability, establishing more formal roles, rejecting deviant ideas and behaviour, and accepting the possibility of absolute truths and the attainment of expertise. High uncertainty avoidance indicates that people like to control the future. It is associated with being dogmatic, authoritarian, traditional and superstitious.

Looking at fifty countries, the uncertainty-avoidance index plotted against the power-distance index reveals several clusters of countries that are characterized by strong uncertainty avoidance and large power distance. Most Latin American and European countries fall into this category but:

- countries such as Singapore, Hong Kong and India combine large power distance with weak uncertainty avoidance, while
- Scandinavian and Anglo-Saxon countries are typically countries with small power distance and weak uncertainty avoidance.

CULTURAL CHARACTERISTICS OF SEVEN EUROPEAN COUNTRIES

On the basis of cross cultural research, Ronen (1986) gives the following brief descriptions of the country-specific characteristics identified in Hofstede's work.

Belgium. Emphasis is on duty but risk tolerance is low. Importance is placed on being sharp-witted; less importance is placed on being tolerant or thoughtful. Belgians are high on uncertainty avoidance, moderate in masculinity and relatively high in power distance.

Germany is low in risk tolerance, with an emphasis on self-realization, leadership and independence as life goals. (West) Germans are highly competitive, with little regard being placed on patience and reliability. They are relatively high on masculinity but low on power distance.

The Netherlands. The Dutch are concerned with expertise and duty, and less concerned with self-realization. They are high in risk tolerance and content to be reactive rather than proactive, with an emphasis on being sharp-witted.

France. The French place strong emphasis on logic and rationality, with stress on individual opinions. Style and energy are essential to organizational success. It is important to be sharp-witted as well as mature, steady and reliable. One-way communication is relatively acceptable. Self-perception is one of tolerance of conflict. France is high on uncertainty avoidance, relatively low on masculinity, and high on power distance.

Italy is low in risk tolerance and high on uncertainty avoidance. Italians are willing to accept affection and warmth but are high on masculinity. They are highly competitive but prefer to use group decision making and are moderate on the power-distance index.

Denmark, like other Scandinavian countries, is above average in risk tolerance; with emphasis on maturity and steadiness and a premium placed on tolerance and sociability. Femininity is combined with weak uncertainty avoidance and low power distance.

Great Britain. Strong social class traditions exist here. Security is an important goal, yet pleasure is emphasized as a life goal. Resourcefulness, logic, and adaptability are considered important; the British people are highly competitive. They are low on indices of power distance and uncertainty avoidance, high on individualism and relatively high on masculinity.

(3) André Laurent

Another striking example of cultural differences appeared in a systematic survey of upper-middle managers attending executive programmes. Participants were asked to respond to the following statement:

> It is important for a manager to have at hand pricise answers to most of the questions that his subordinates may raise about their work.

Responses were scored on a five-point scale from 'strongly agree' to 'strongly disagree'. The results show that

- Only a minority (13 per cent) of both Swedish and American managers agreed with the above statement.
- A majority (59 per cent) of both French and Italian managers agreed.
- Between 30 and 50 per cent of managers from Great Britain, Germany, Switzerland and Belgium agreed with the statement.

So, whereas most French and Italian managers expect the boss to have the answers, American and Swedes apparently do not. As a result, French and Italian managers must often pretend to know more than their subordinates even if they do not. If they are found to know less than their subordinates about the task, their authority base could suffer and their credibility may be lost.

(4) Michael Bond

Recent work by Michael Bond shows some clear national cultural differences in people's attitudes to time. He analysed data from a questionnaire, designed with a deliberate Eastern bias, to measure the values of students in 23 countries. From this data he was able to reproduce three of the factors identified by Hofstede, but he also found a fourth factor unrelated to anything found by Hofstede. He named it '*Confucian Dynamism*', referring to a long-term versus short-term orientation in society and to whether one is mainly preoccupied with the future or the past. Bond chose the name 'Confucian' because nearly all of the values seemed to be taken straight from the teachings of Confucius. His research suggests that:

- People with a short-term orientation emphasize the values of perseverance, ordering relationships by status, thrift and having a sense of shame.

- By contrast, people with a long-term orientation stress personal steadiness and stability, protecting your 'face', respect for tradition, and reciprocation of greetings, favours and gifts.

After positioning 23 nationalities on the Confucian dimension, Bond found that

- West Europeans and North Americans have a short-term orientation and concern for the past.

- In contrast, most East Asians have a long-term orientation and are more concerned with the future.

- Some non-Asian countries such as Brazil and the Netherlands also score relatively high on this Confucian dimension.

- Great Britain, Canada, Nigeria and Pakistan are the most short-term oriented countries.

The way in which societies look at time also differs in the Trompenaars study. He points out that, in some societies, what somebody has achieved in the past is not that important. It is more important to know what plans they have developed for the future. In other societies you can make more of an impression with your past accomplishments than those of today.

These cultural differences greatly influence corporate activities.

To measure these cultural differences in relation to time, Trompenaars asked his respondents to draw three circles representing the past, present and future. He found that:

- In some cultures, such as Russia, the typical response is to draw three separate circles; indicating no connection between the past, present and future, though the future is considered more important than the past and the present (as indicated by the size of the circles).

- Belgians typically see a very small overlap between the present and the past. In this they are not dissimilar to the British who have a rather stronger link with the past but see it as relatively unimportant.

- The French are different again. For them all three time zones overlap considerably.

- The Germans think the present and the future are strongly interrelated.

Key questions for assessing cultural differences

For assessing individualism:

- Is everyone expected to look after himself or herself and his or her immediate family members?
- Are people expected to be loyal to one group or organization?
- Do people have considerable freedom to select the jobs that they do?
- Are hiring, rewarding and promotion decisions in organizations based largely on individual needs, achievements and responsibilities?
- Do individual interests prevail over collective interests?
- Does everyone have a right to privacy, to own property and to express an opinion?

For assessing uncertainty avoidance:

- Do members of this specific society feel threatened by uncertain or unknown situations?
- Are people allowed to express anger, aggression and other emotions?
- Are formal rules and procedures considered essential and absolute?
- Are people allowed to disagree openly with superiors?
- Are deviant behaviours and ideas considered irrational and dangerous?
- Is conflict considered an unnecessary evil that should be eliminated?

For assessing status/power differences:

- Is power based on family background, gender, age and/or ability to use force?
- Do the prevailing ideologies and belief systems emphasize hierarchy and stratification?

- Does the law stress or guarantee that everybody has equal rights, regardless of status?
- Are inequalities between people both expected and desired?
- Are status symbols and privileges for the powerful popular?
- Do employees expect to obey their bosses, regardless of the consequences?

For assessing time perceptions:

- Is punctuality considered a virtue? Is it important to keep appointments strictly, to schedule meetings in advance and not arrive late?
- Are people mainly preoccupied with the future or with the past and the present?
- Are tasks and deadlines scheduled very tightly, with thin time slots between activities?
- Are activities typically scheduled and undertaken one at a time (sequential orientation), or do people usually engage in more than one activity at a time (synchronic orientation)?
- Is time considered short and expensive, or rather infinite and flexible?

For assessing the importance of personal relationships:

- Are personal relationships more important than formal rules and regulations?
- Are good friends expected to take care of each other, regardless of the costs?
- Are business contracts based on informal networks and private understandings.
- Do people seek and expect to get personal favours and pull levers privately through direct relationships, especially relationships to the leader?
- Are relationships typically close and long-lasting?

What are the implications of these differences for negotiating with other cultures?

(1) We are not aware of our cultural bias
Although people generally recognize the existence of cultural differences, most of us do not recognize our own peculiar way of behaving as being influenced, if not determined, by cultural habits and assumptions. Because we learn cultural behaviour early in life, it frequently affects us on an unconscious level.

(2)   We become blind to our own cultural norms
Laurent points out that our own cultural traits are so much part of
ourselves that we cannot see them any more. As we become blind to
our own cultural norms, we often assume others to be similar to
ourselves and we become greatly surprised (and most often upset)
when others, coming from different cultures, do not behave or act as
we do. *Cultural myopia* – the inability to see one's own cultural
make-up – leads to implicit ethnocentrism in management, a
tendency to hold one's own way as being the best and to expect it
from, or to impose it on, others.

*(3)   Other cultures are implicitly perceived as unfortunate deviations from
the norm (the norm being obviously that of our own culture)*
Webber (1969) has articulated this point. As he put it 'Most of us act,
think and dream in terms of the norms and standards we have
absorbed from the culture in which we are reared. That which our
culture values, we value; that which our culture abhors, we abhor.
By education or experience some of us become aware that there are
other values and beliefs that make sense too – as much or more than
our own. But we see them hazily and all too often, with age, the
awareness slips away. A few, a very few, are able to escape,
overcome parochialism and see the world more objectively. But
escape is by no means entirely desirable. We can feel alone and
unsure when the comfortable values of our old culture fall away,
become irrelevant and are replaced by nothing'.

(4)   Stereotyping is common
The tendency to hold one's own way as being the best and to expect
the same from others is often reinforced by stereotypes of other
cultures and nationalities. For instance, in the interaction between
Germans and Americans, certain stereotypes recur with a high
degree of predictability. As Hofstede (1991) notes 'Americans see
Germans as logical, thorough, well educated, but also as distant,
cold, and brooding. Germans see Americans as friendly, open,
flexible, but also as insincere, uncritical and shallow'.
    While the existence of such stereotypes can prevent serious
misunderstanding between different cultural groups, they can be
very misleading. As Adler (1986) says 'The French, in describing the
British as "perfidious", "hypocritical" and "vague", are in fact
describing the Englishman's typical lack of a general model, or
theory, and his preference for a more pragmatic, evolutionary
approach. This is hard for the Frenchman to believe, let alone accept
for a viable alternative, until, working alongside one another, the

Frenchman comes to see that there is usually no ulterior motive behind the Englishman's vagueness, but rather a capacity to think aloud and adapt to circumstances. For his part, the Englishman comes to see that, far from being "distant", "superior" or "out of touch with reality", the Frenchman's concern for a general model or theory is what lends vision, focus and cohesion to an enterprise or project, as well as leadership and much needed authority'.

How can you be effective as an international negotiator?

To be effective in international negotiations, you must be aware of your own and the opponent's cultural biases and learn to set them aside (or at least take them into account) when faced with different cultural groups. Awareness of cultural differences does not necessarily mean that you can easily overcome their effects; however, knowledge at least provides a chance to avoid some of the problems that result from cultural blindness.

The following checklist, which is based on Geert Hofstede's original culture assessment survey, lets you test your cultural biases in a structured fashion.

TESTING CULTURAL ASSUMPTIONS

Question 1: In your view, which countries have the highest percentage of people agreeing with the following 25 statements?

Question 2: Which countries have the lowest percentage of people agreeing?

1. It is important for a manager to have at hand precise answers to most of the questions that his subordinates may raise about their work.

2. Most organizations would be better off if conflict could be eliminated forever.

3. When the respective roles of the members of a department become complex, detailed job descriptions are a useful way of clarifying responsibilities.

4. An organizational structure in which certain subordinates have two direct bosses should be avoided at all costs.

5. Inequalities among people should be minimized.

6. The ideal boss is a benevolent autocrat or a good father.

7. The average human being has an inherent dislike of work and will avoid it if he can.

8. There are few qualities in a man more admirable than dedication and loyalty to his company.

9. Employees should not disagree openly with their boss.

10. Decisions made by individuals are usually of better quality than decisions made by groups.

11. Interesting work is not as important as earnings.

12. In life everyone is supposed to take care of him or herself and his immediate family.

13. Everyone has a right to have a private life and to express an opinion.

14. Organizational interests are a legitimate reason for interfering with people's private lives.

15. Our culture places a lot of emphasis on individual initiative and achievement.

16. Punctuality and meeting deadlines is very important.

17. Deviant ideas and behaviours are not easily tolerated.

18. There is a strong sense of nationalism in our country.

19. People who break the law should be punished.

20. Most people worry a lot about the future.

21. A good manager is aggressive, competitive, firm and decisive.

22. The expression of emotion is a weakness that interferes with effective business processes.

23. Money and property are more important than family life and social relationships.

24. Men are expected to make a career; those who don't see themselves as failures.

25. Men occupy all important positions in this society.

Scoring

According to Hofstede's results, the answers are as follows:

For statements 1 to 9 (power distance):
  Highest percentage in France, Turkey, Belgium, Philippines, Singapore.
  Lowest percentage in Israel, Denmark, Ireland, New Zealand, Norway.

For statements 10 to 15 (individualism):
  Highest percentage in Australia, Ireland, Italy, UK, India.
  Lowest percentage in Portugal, Sweden, Japan, Chile, Germany.

For statements 16 to 20 (uncertainty avoidance):
Highest percentage in Greece, Portugal, Spain, Japan, France, Belgium.
Lowest percentage in Singapore, Hong Kong, India, UK, North America.

For statements 21 to 25 (masculinity/achievement):
Highest percentage in Austria, Japan, Italy, Switzerland, Venezuela.
Lowest percentage in Scandinavia, Netherlands, Spain, France, Thailand.

Adopting culture-specific strategies

What is true on one side of the Pyrenees, is not on the other.
(Pascal, 1623–1662)

The previous sections have offered some examples of cultural differences between nations. Although most people are aware of these differences, managers involved in international negotiations often view them at best as a handicap to effective problem solving. As a result they continue to adhere to the theory of uniformity and universality – some single best way of doing things – when it comes to managing their intercultural negotiations.

However, identical negotiation strategies and tactics may have different effects in different countries. Because of this, it is useful to look briefly at some of the strategies and techniques which work best in different cultures. At the risk of over-simplification, this section offers some tips for negotiating in four types of cultures.

In achievement-oriented cultures

- Make sure you or someone in your negotiation team has enough technical knowledge and experience to convince the other party that your proposals will work.
- Respect the need of the other party to look strong, competent and experienced. To challenge their professionalism is likely to cause resentment and retaliation.
- Use professional titles and qualifications to underline your competence and personal achievements.

In status-oriented cultures

- Make sure your negotiation team has enough older or senior members with formal roles and status in society. Sending a young, albeit brilliant, representative to an ascriptive culture, like India or China, is likely to be perceived as an insult by the Indian or Chinese negotiators.

  As Trompenaars points out, it is quite upsetting for people in status-oriented cultures when they have to negotiate with young, aggressive men and women, who spout knowledge as if it were a kind of ammunition before which the other side is expected to surrender.

- Respect the line of hierarchy in the other negotiation team. Do not undermine the credibility of the most senior member (who is very often the spokesperson), even if you suspect he does not have the necessary background. Keep in mind that in many parts of the world, when dealing with someone of the same or higher level, it is customary to say in public that the other person would like to hear rather than give the facts.

- Use titles and symbols to indicate your status in society. For this reason, the Japanese always exchange business cards before conversations begin.

- Dress conservatively. Do not use first names. Refrain from joking and social chatting. Avoid negotiating over the phone or by mail; it is considered more polite, or effective, to do business face-to-face.

In future-oriented cultures

- Avoid displays of impatience. Expect and accept prolonged periods of no movement during the negotiation. Americans, being particularly short-term oriented, often expect negotiations to take a minimum amount of time. This sense of urgency disadvantages them with regard to their less hurried opponents from future cultures, such as Brazil, Singapore and Taiwan. For instance, one Brazilian company invited a group of American negotiators to discuss a contract renewal one week before it expired, knowing that Americans will make more concessions as they approach their self-imposed deadline.

- Spend more time on interpersonal relationships during your negotiation. People from future-oriented societies often rely on personal respect and friendship, rather than on legal systems, to enforce contracts. They emphasize the relationship, not the written agreement. Hence, consider the impact of your claims and proposals on the long-term relationship with the other party.

- Reciprocation of greetings, gifts and personal favours is a social ritual that is very important in future-oriented cultures. Concerns with costs, winning, and 'face saving' are generally subordinate to maintaining personal relationships.

In uncertainty-avoidance (UA) cultures

- Natives from countries with a strong need for uncertainty avoidance (such as Germany, Belgium and France) feel threatened by ambiguous or unknown situations. When they buy something, they expect it to be presented in an orderly fashion and extensively described. Therefore, when negotiating with people from this type of culture, it is wise to be fully prepared as they demand that all the details be at hand.

Key points for negotiating across cultures

1. *Planning is crucial.* Before entering negotiations, learn sufficient about the culture of the people you are going to negotiate with, their customs, norms, values and practices.

2. *Beware of making cultural assumptions.* Stereotypes can be misleading in the sense that no two human beings belonging to the same culture are going to be exactly the same.

3. *Be flexible.* Adapt your negotiating styles, strategies and tactics to the specific people, issues and circumstances.

4. *Language is an important link across cultures* and between negotiators, but it also can be a barrier. Sometimes similar words have different meanings in different languages. Therefore, check understanding frequently during the negotiation by summarizing and asking open questions.

5. *Non-verbal communication is a very important factor* in intercultural negotiation. Be careful about your own body language and the meaning attached to the other party's gestures, tone of voice, silences and facial expressions.

6. *Negotiating styles differ significantly across cultures.* The cultural context also largely determines who should be a member of the negotiation team, who is the team leader, and how and when the negotiation should be conducted. Understanding these differences is critical if one is to avoid silly mistakes.

- The emotional need for rules and regulations in a strong UA culture demands a considerable sense of punctuality. Keep appointments strictly, schedule meetings in advance and do not be late. Discuss one issue at a time. Avoid interruptions and delays.

- High UA also leads to a strong need for formality. In Germany, Japan and other countries it is proper to address people using their formal titles. Critical comments about situations, conditions and people are never made in public. Such informality would severely insult their sense of propriety and self-respect.

- People from high UA cultures have the reputation for being hard bargainers. They habitually use extreme opening demands and make small concessions. Haggling is common, expected and an essential part of the game.

REVIEW QUESTIONS

1. Using the key questions for assessing cultural differences listed in this chapter, what are the key factors you should take into account in preparing to negotiate with people from the following cultural backgrounds:

- French
- Italian
- South American
- Danish

2. Considering the research findings of Trompenaars, Hofstede and others, what are the likely problems that may occur in merger negotiaitons between the following two companies:

- A French versus a Swedish orginization.
- A North American versus a German organization.
- A Japanese versus a British organization.

3. Think of a recent situation where you have negotiated with a person from a different cultural background.

- What were your expectations before the meeting?
- What surprised you? Why?

- Identify three things you could have done differently in order to make the communication between you and the other parties more effective.
- What else could you have done to improve the outcome?

CASE STUDY: BORG-WARNER CHEMICALS

Introduction
This case was writen by Juliet Burdet-Taylor, Research Associate at the International Institute for Management Development, under the supervision of Professor Christopher Parker, as a basis for class discussion rather than to illustrate either effective or ineffective handling of international negotiations.

After reading this case, ask yourself:

1. What are the most important differences between the French and Americans in this negotiation?
2. What caused these differences?
3. How would you assess the effectiveness of the negotiators in dealing with the cultural differences between the two parties?
4. What lessons do you draw from this case for negotiation across cultures?

Background
George McNally, President of Borg-Warner Chemicals worldwide, picked up the telephone. 'Al, hi there! Good to hear your voice . . . Oh really, is that so, a large ABS plant in France for sale. Well we certainly need more capacity.' McNally fired off questions into the phone, making rapid notes as he listened to Al Watson, President of Amsterdam-based Borg-Warner Chemicals Europe. Watson's voice fairly crackled with enthusiasm. 'Get down there as soon as you can and let me know what it looks like' said McNally.

The Borg-Warner Corporation
In 1985, the chemical division of the three billion dollar Borg-Warner Corporation was the company's biggest money maker and its ABS (acrylonitrile butadiene styrene) engineering thermoplastic, 'Cycolac', was world leader with over one third of the market. Cycolac, which accounted for 80 per cent of the chemical division's business, was used in the manufacture of computer housings, telephones and automotive parts and trim, and its users included firms such as Ford, Apple, IBM, Philips and Electrolux. Borg-Warner attributed Cycolac's world-leading position not only to the product's superior technical properties but also to the level of service given to the client in design, conceptualization and

engineering during the product development phase. Although it was traditional for thermoplastics suppliers to be involved at design phase of a new product, Borg-Warner Chemicals felt they had a clear edge over their competitors in this function. To achieve such levels of service orientation, the firm made heavy use of 'management by objectives' techniques to set priorities and assess the performance of individual employees.

Borg-Warner Chemicals Europe (BWCE)

Al Watson ran Borg-Warner's European operations from Amsterdam, where the company's European research and development laboratories and an ABS plant were also located. Most of the managers who reported directly to Watson were relatively young, and Watson, an American in his sixties with a lifetime's experience in the chemicals and plastics business, was something of a father figure and mentor to these managers. Watson's experience and astuteness had made him one of the most respected executives in the Borg-Warner Corporation.

Sales Director, Herman de Groot, was responsible for the four regional sales offices in Europe, and the managers of the two European ABS plants, in Holland and in Scotland, reported to Hans Munting, Director of Operations. Although able to produce 85 000 tons of ABS per year, by 1984 both plants were nearing capacity, a situation which was causing some concern to Borg-Warner Chemicals' management.

The European ABS market

Rivalry in the European ABS market was intense. Eight large companies vied for market share, with Borg-Warner and Bayer fighting for the number-one slot. France's top producer of ABS was state-owned CdF Chimie. Price wars were common as firms fought to increase their market position, many adopting price-cutting tactics in markets, such as France, where they did not have a production operation.

The demand for a new generation of high-quality, glossy ABS grades forced producers to adopt superior technology and develop thermoplastics that could be used in shiny, more expensive electrical appliances, such as mixers, hair driers, etc. Market-share gains depended on producers' ability to manufacture these sophisticated plastics which required both HRG (high rubber graft) technology, as well as SAN (styrene acrylonitrile) technology. Borg-Warner Chemicals Europe was using HRG but not SAN. To develop this technology themselves would take five or six years so they would have no alternative but to purchase some critical raw materials from their competitors or lose the race for market share.

The European competitive situation caused Borg-Warner Corporation to hesitate before making new investments in Europe until some rationalization had taken place. In the US ABS market, Borg-Warner with approximately 55 per cent market share, had only two major competitors.

The site

About 60 kilometres northwest of Paris in the pastoral Oise region of Picardie, near Beauvais, is a small town called Villers St. Sépulcre (VSS). The narrow and fast-flowing River Thérain that runs through the area had been used for centuries to provide energy in the region. Various industrial activities had been carried out on the site over the years and in May 1960, workshops were opened to manufacture butadiene copolymers, using a process developed by U.S. Rubber (Uniroyal). This ABS material, sold under the name 'Kralastic', was one of Cycolac's first competitors.

Over the next 20 years, the site moved in and out of the hands of four other owners, mainly huge French nationalized companies. The last owner but one was PCUK, a company created by the merger of two of France's oldest industrial concerns, Pechiney and Ugine Kuhlmann, active respectively in metallurgy and chemicals. When President Mitterrand came to power in 1981, France's chemical industry was reorganized. PCUK was nationalized in 1982, its loss ridden chemical division was spun off, and parts were taken over by CdF Chimie (the chemical division of the state coal company, Charbonnage de France (CdF)), which had consolidated sales of FF25.7 billion in 1984 (approximately $3 billion). The VSS plant fell into the hands of CdF Chimie's ABS division and became an almost independent company. In 1984 CdF had a share of more than 30 per cent of the French ABS market and was particularly strong in the automotive sector, selling to Renault and Peugeot, each of which had been instrumental in the development with the VSS technical team of CdF's highly successful 'Ugikral' line of products. These two major automotive manufacturers, who together consumed about one-third of the total ABS produced in France, bought most of their ABS requirements from CdF Chimie. CdF Chimie's VSS plant was the only ABS producer in France.

The Americans acquisition team

'Roses are blooming in Picardie' Jim Parker said, looking at a signpost through the window of the Citroen station-wagon. Sam Gore, a younger American looked puzzled. 'Favourite song with the boys during the war' Parker explained. 'That's right' said the third man, who was Dutch. 'This is Picardie. The area was full of troops in 1944.' 'A nightingale sang in Berkeley Square' said Gore, laughing. 'That was no nightingale' his colleague pointed out 'That was a canary. Fattest bird I've ever seen. Funny to see it singing in its cage right in the middle of a chemicals plant.' Hans Munting, Director of Operations for Borg-Warner Chemicals Europe, was driving back to Paris with two members of Borg-Warner Chemical's acquisition team from the U.S. after visiting CdF's ABS plant at VSS. The atmosphere in the car was relaxed as the three men discussed the day's visit. Sam Gore turned towards the Dutchman, smiling. 'That crazy bird sitting in its cage; it must be hard for you to see a thing like that, Hans, with all your sophisticated security drills! We go through a whole procedure of doublechecking for contamination, with our electronic lock-out systems and so forth, while they just lower a canary into a reactor and if it survives, in they go. I know it's an old mining tradition but it's amazing how these things vary from country to country!'

Jim Parker had started jotting down numbers on a note pad. 'Interesting day. Best thing we've seen so far. Enormous ABS potential.' He pushed the paper towards the Dutchman. 'Combining our three operations would give us 150–170 000 metric tons a year. That's about 30 per cent of European capacity. With their 450 or so employees, we'd have about 1200 people in all. Pretty good, Hans, right?' Munting, who had been scribbling notes and making sketches on his pad since the three men got into the car, nodded and showed his sheet of paper to the two Americans.

'Here's how it could be: monomer storage, polymerization, coagulation, drying and compounding – separate buildings.' Munting was outlining the phases of ABS manufacture. 'Then we have effluent treatment, utilities and maintenance areas, and here the resin and weigh silos.' He pointed to the plan with his finger. 'OK, there's a lot to be done. Maintenance needs more structure. They seem to have outside contractors all over the place. Obviously, some of these older buildings will have to be replaced. The place is run down, but there's so much space. That's what counts for us . . . huge site with plenty of room to build.'

Jim Parker drew dollar signs on his pad. 'It certainly is run-down . . . Quite an investment needed to bring it into line. What do you think, Hans? I'd say it's money well spent myself.' 'I'm excited' the Dutchman replied. 'The site is unkempt but their R&D surprised me. They're installing SAN which is definitely a point in their favour. Quite an impressive technical team. Their colours are good, too, even on those old machines and with practically no quality control.' He hesitated, then went on 'Certain things are different for sure, but . . .' The younger American laughed again. 'You mean that crazy canary? That bird is sort of symbolic, Hans. It says something about our attitudes and theirs. Very interesting.'

'I can tell you right now' said Munting, who had been involved in bringing BWCE's safety standards up to prize-winning levels 'if we take over that plant, the first one to get early retirement is that canary. You can't take risks with ABS production. If a reactor explodes, you're in trouble.'

'They'd done their homework though' continued Munting, who knew the European ABS business inside out. 'They know their competitors and they've worked out what we have and they haven't. I'm optimistic in spite of the state of the place. Sure, the area is depressed and the plant is losing money. The whole group is losing money. The government has lost interest. Their working conditions are pretty rough by our standards.

The previous four or five owners did not do much for them. But some of those plant people have worked there all their lives. There's a guy in maintenance with 40 years of service.'

The French
Later on the same afternoon, when the visitors had left the plant, André Farrer, Works Manager at VSS, Jean-Pierre Tortai, head of the research laboratory and Alain Hermet, Operations Manager, met with Jacques Roudeix, Commercial Director at VSS, and Etienne Saix of CdF Chimie's Paris-based long-range planning department. Saix had been responsible for the research work on potential merger partners for CdF.

'*Ils sont intéressés* . . . They are interested' Saix said. 'And I think we should be interested too.' He turned towards the men across the table. Jean-Pierre Tortai, burly and bearded, fiddled with a small glass jar as he spoke. 'It's not that we're not interested, Etienne. It's more a question of the differences between us. Will they understand what we've done in R&D?' Tortai unscrewed the top of the jar allowing some coloured pellets to spill onto his hand. They gave off the same acrid chemical odour that could be smelled all over the site. This was the ABS plastic produced at VSS which, packed in 50-lb sacks, would be shipped off to converters for moulding or extrusion to finish up as parts for consumer durables or computer housings. Tortai was a brilliant researcher, sensitive and justly proud of his achievements. CdF had been slow in rewarding him for his work.

'I know Americans are different' replied Saix 'but let's do everything we can to keep going – maintain our research team, our customers, our whole set-up.' Saix paused and continued. 'Look at it like this. There are too many ABS producers in Europe, and there's no future for small companies in the engineering thermoplastic business. Big money is needed for investment in R&D for new generations of products. To succeed in a diversified market like Europe, you must have strong marketing and sales as well as plenty of funds to invest. As you know, CdF has been looking for a suitable partner for quite a while. We have been hoping to find one that would agree to a merger rather than a straight takeover.'

'We must try to do three things for CdF Chimie: rebuild the profitability of the business, preserve our development target for ABS and protect employment here on the site' said Saix, looking at the faces of the men across the table. 'Borg-Warner Chemicals is the biggest ABS manufacturer in the world. I think they could help us on all counts. The main difference would be that a U.S. company would own us, or part of us. Believe me, I prefer this solution to one or two of the others open to us. BW is a decent U.S. conglomerate. Sure, they are profit oriented. They make money. They can afford to invest in us, in the plant, in our people and our research. I know they're American, but if we want to keep the plant open, it's just about the only solution we have.'

Farrer, who had been listening to Saix, stood up and walked to the window. 'It's not the Americans that bother me' he said. 'They would probably leave us alone as long as they get their results. It's the people in the middle. Do we want the Dutch interfering with our systems and telling our people what to do, probably going right over our heads?' Saix sensed that Farrer was worried about losing his power. It was felt that Farrer, as site manager, had built himself his own little empire.

'And another thing' Farrer went on 'American companies come and go like the wind. Here today, gone tomorrow. What sort of security is that?'. Before Saix could reply to Farrer, Alain Hermet cut in. Twenty years on the site under three different owners had given Hermet some insights on mergers. When CdF had taken over from PCUK (the previous owners), the management at VSS had breathed a sigh of relief. At the time, the change had been for the better on all levels. But things had changed again, and Hermet was prepared to believe that the arrival of Borg-Warner would not necessarily be negative for CdF in VSS.

'*C'est sûr qu'ils sont différents*' said Hermet 'but as Etienne says, we need them and they want to invest in us. Sometimes being different is a good thing. Maybe we can complement each other. Do we want to see the plant closed? It doesn't make any difference how brilliant your research is if you don't sell your products at a profit. How long have we been losing money here, how long? We are the only French producer of ABS. And we're close to the marketplace. They don't have a few hundred alternatives to choose from and certainly no one with 35 per cent of one of the biggest markets in Europe.' 'And our R&D capacity' said Tortai. 'Our R&D, our products and our customers' said Roudeix, a French ABS veteran, who had spent 13 years with PCUK in operations and R&D before CdF came along. 'And our sales network as well. I agree with Etienne. We have something to offer these people. They liked our research and our colour impressed them too.' Tortai looked up, screwed the cap back on his glass jar and put it on the table. Farrer continued to stare out of the window.

Driving back to Paris, Saix thought over the events of the day. The Borg-Warner visitors had seemed impressed by what they had seen at VSS. Comparing notes on synergy, Saix felt he saw eye to eye with Borg-Warner. They seemed to have come up with findings very similar to his own in their search for a suitable merger partner. The meeting afterwards with the French team had not been easy. Technical people could be inflexible, willing to fight change to the last. If it all went through, there would certainly be some changes. From Saix's point of view, a merger or takeover would be a piece of successful strategy. But the people on site with their different frames of reference would not be easy to convince. Farrer would have a job adjusting. Tortai as well, perhaps. Tortai was a key man who, like many talented R&D experts, was interested mainly in technical questions. Hermet seemed positive about the whole thing. As a strategic planner, the synergies were clear to Saix. Surely the VSS team would come around. They were aware of the vulnerability of their ABS business and that without new capital the plant would probably not survive.

Saix thought about the meeting he had organized with CdF's president and some of its area directors in Paris to discuss Borg-Warner's interest in CdF ABS. After he had outlined what he felt to be the areas of basic synergy, one of the directors had said 'Must it be an American company with headquarters in Holland? There must be somebody French.'

The decision

After meeting with Hans Munting and the two Americans, Al Watson flew to Paris and visited the VSS site with Hans and Wim Broekhuysen, Director, Human Resources of BWCE. 'Well, Wim, if we go for it, you'll be in charge of getting a lot of things organized for these people' said Watson as they walked round the site. 'It's going to be a challenge, but I'll back you up.' Broekhuysen, whose French was already quite fluent, chatted to plant workers and personnel as they went round. He wanted to start off on the right foot with the French. He knew there would be plenty of problems to solve. Absenteeism in the plant was high. Workers mistrusted management, and there was little dialogue between them. But his greatest worry was the idea of dealing with the labour unions. There were 5 or 6 on site, including the powerful communist CGT (Confédération Générale de Travail).

'No helmets, protective glasses, emergency showers, or eye-baths on the site' said Hans Munting as he and Watson watched a shift come out of the factory. 'You'll have your work cut out putting our safety standards in here, Hans, if we come' said the president. 'I know' said Munting. 'They had 12 lost time accidents last year.' Looking at the dilapidated building the workers used to change their clothes, Watson turned to Broekhuysen. 'If we do get this place, Wim, what would you do first, rebuild the office block or the changing room?' Broekhuysen, a conscientious and disciplined manager, was scribbling eagerly on his notepad. His list of things to be done was already several pages long.

Back in Holland, Al Watson phoned George McNally, President of Borg-Warner Chemicals, Parkersburg, West Virginia. 'We're on to something, George' said Watson to his boss. 'CdF's ABS plant, near Beauvais . . . 65 hectares in the rolling countryside of Picardie, one hour from Charles de Gaulle airport, just off a throughway, good rail connections. The area's depressed and the workers look down in the mouth. There's a lot to be done . . . new buildings, new machinery, a total clean-up. Quality and safety are way below Borg-Warner's levels. But technically they're good. Hans agrees with me. Of course, the French are different. Language will be tough. But if we don't go for it, someone else will.' As he spoke, Watson heard McNally flipping through the pages of his diary. 'I'd like to come over and see it' said the president. 'It seems to fit in with our plans. We could become the largest European ABS producer, with a third of the market.'

The deal

Months of complex negotiations followed, and lawyers from the United States and several European countries thrashed out the conditions of an agreement. Twelve countries were involved in the deal, many with different local laws. It took some time to come to a suitable agreement, but it was finally decided that Borg-Warner and CdF Chimie would each own part of the newly-formed Borg-Warner Chemicals Europe B.V. that would be run from Amsterdam. Borg-Warner would be the majority shareholder with 70 per cent, and CdF would hold the remaining 30 per cent. This new company would handle the French operation at VSS (to be referred to as Beaumar), the Dutch operation (known as Holmar) and the Scottish operation (known as Grangemar). On January 16, 1986, Borg-Warner Chemicals' representatives sat with CdF's team and a group of lawyers. It took them nine hours to review and sign the 46 separate documents that would marry the two partners.

The merger agreement stipulated that the new company's management would be made up of representatives of the two companies in proportion to assets each brought to the venture. Borg-Warner would name the president and CdF an executive vice-president. Al Watson was named President and Etienne Saix, who joined the soon-to-be founded company several months before the deal was finalized, was nominated by CdF Chimie to the management group of Borg-Warner Chemicals Europe B.V. As Executive Vice-President, reporting to Al Watson, Saix was to be responsible for long-range planning.

Bibliography

Acuff, F. L. and Villere, M. *Games Negotiators Play*, Business Horizons, February 1976.

Adler, N. *International Dimensions of Organizational Behavior*, Boston: Kent Publishing Company, 1986.

Atkinson, G. *The Effective Negotiator*, London: Quest Research Publications, 1975.

Fisher, R. and Ury, W. *Getting to Yes*, Boston: Houghton Mifflin, 1981.

Hofstede, G. *Culture's Consequences*, Beverly Hills: Sage Publications, 1980.

Hofstede, G. *Cultures and Organizations*, London: McGraw-Hill, 1991.

Illich, J. *Deal-Breakers and Breakthroughs*, New York: Wiley, 1992.

Janis, I. *Victims of Groupthink: A Psychological Study of Foreign Policy Decisions and Fiascos* (second edition), Boston: Houghton Mifflin, 1982.

Jones, J. E. and Pfeiffer, J. W. *The 1973 Annual Handbook for Group Facilitators*, San Diego: University Associates, 1973.

Kennedy, G. *Pocket Negotiator*, London: The Economist Books, 1993.

Laurent, A. 'Matrix Organizations and Latin Cultures', *International Studies of Management and Organization*, 1981, **10** (4), p.101–14.

Lewicki, R. J. and Litterer, J. A. *Negotiation: Readings, Excercises, and Cases*, Homewood: Irwin, 1985.

Pruitt, D. and Carnevale, P. *Negotiation in Social Conflict*, Buckingham: Open University Press, 1993.

Pruitt, D. and Rubin, J. *Social Conflict: Escalation, Stalemate and Settlement*, New York: McGraw-Hill, 1986.

Ronen, S. *Comparative and Multinational Management*, New York: Wiley, 1986.

Taylor, D. and Wright, P. *Developing Interpersonal Skills through Tutored Practice*, London: Prentice Hall, 1988.

Thomas, K. W. 'Towards multidimensional values in teaching: the example of conflict behaviours', *Academy of Management Review*, July 1977, p. 487.

Thomas, K. and Kilmann, R. *Conflict Mode Instrument*, Tuxedo, NY: XICOM. Inc., 1974.

Trompenaars, F. *Riding the Waves of Culture*, London: The Economist Books, 1993.

Vanover, M. 'Getting Things Done through Coalitions', *Leadership*, American Society of Association Executives, 1980.

Webber, R. H. 'Convergence or divergence', *Columbia Journal of World Business*, 1969, **4** (3), pp. 75–83.

Whetten, D. and Cameron, K. *Developing Management Skills*, New York: HarperCollins, 1991.

Appendix

The Critical Mistakes Most Managers Make

1. Entering negotiations with a preset mindset.

2. Not knowing who has final negotiating authority.

3. Not knowing what power they have and how to use it.

4. Starting negotiations with only a general and final goal.

5. Failing to advance positions and arguments of substance.

6. Losing control over unimportant factors.

7. Failing to let the other side make the first offer.

8. Ignoring time and location as negotiating factors.

9. Giving up when things seem to be deadlocked.

10. Not knowing when to close.

Negotiations often fail for predictable reasons

The most common include:

- The "One-Track" syndrome

- The "Win-Lose" syndrome

- The "Random Walk" syndrome

- The "Conflict Avoidance" syndrome

- The "Time Capsule" syndrome

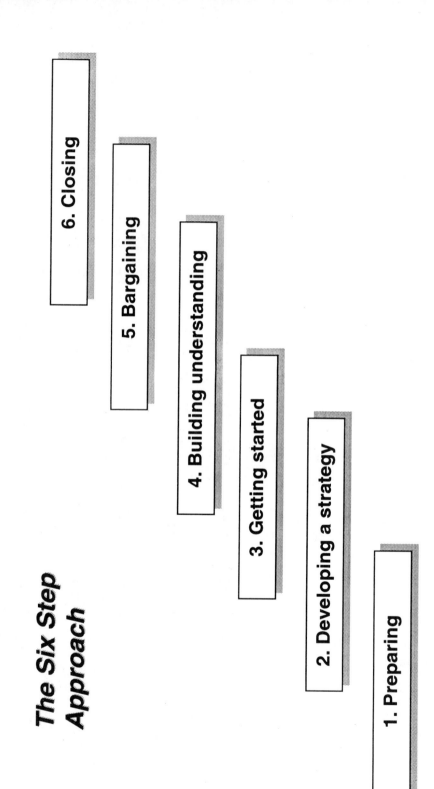

The Six Step Approach

1. Preparing

2. Developing a strategy

3. Getting started

4. Building understanding

5. Bargaining

6. Closing

The First Step of Negotiation

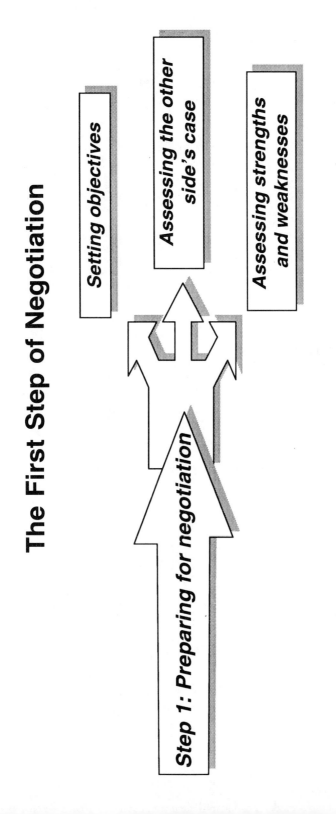

Setting objectives

Assessing the other side's case

Assessing strengths and weaknesses

Step 1: Preparing for negotiation

How to Set Your Bargaining Objectives

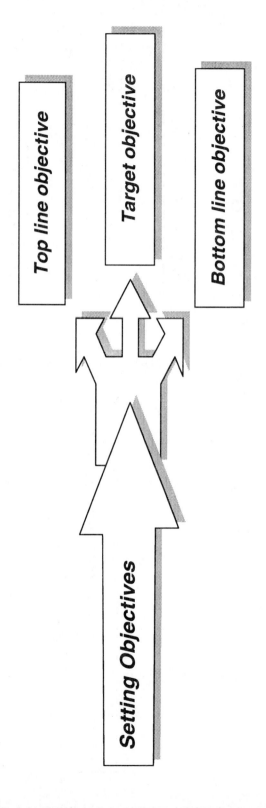

Top line objective

Target objective

Bottom line objective

Setting Objectives

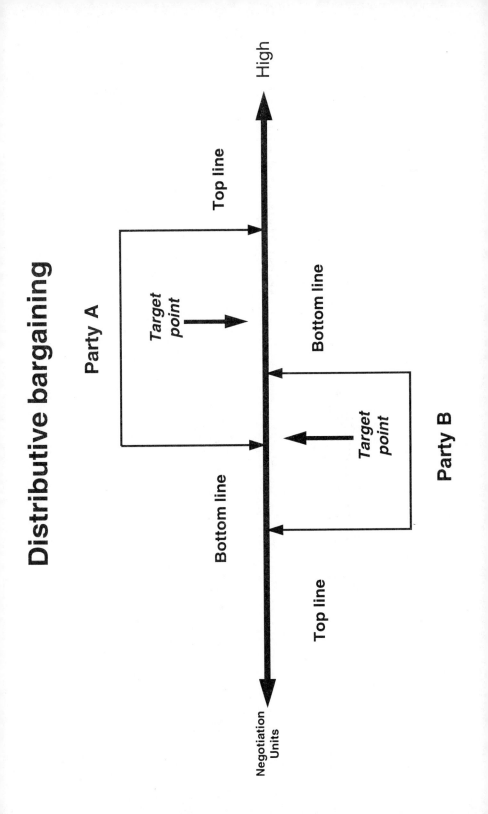

Distributive bargaining

Negotiation Units

High

Party A

Top line

Target point

Bottom line

Bottom line

Target point

Top line

Party B

The Second Step of Negotiation

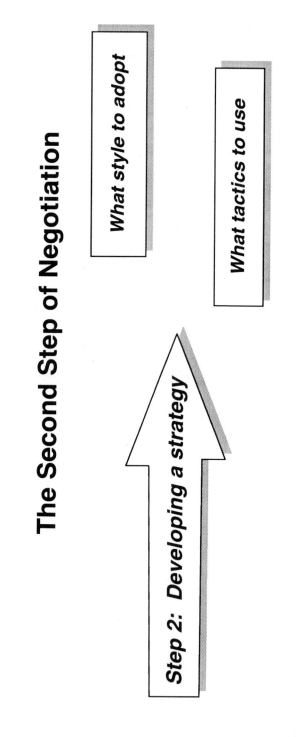

What style to adopt

What tactics to use

Step 2: Developing a strategy

Five Negotiating Styles

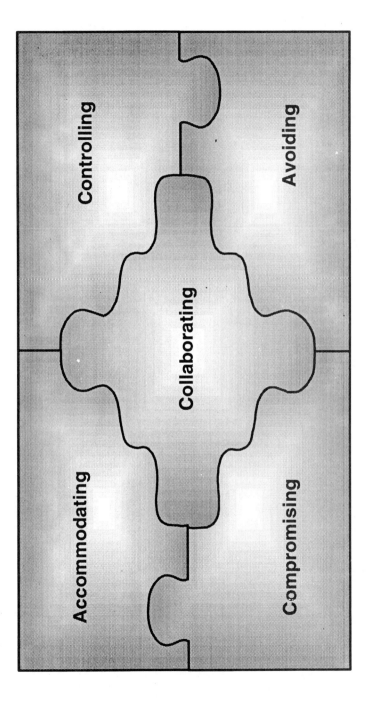

Determining Your Negotiating Style Profile

Transfer the total score for each style to the appropriate column below:

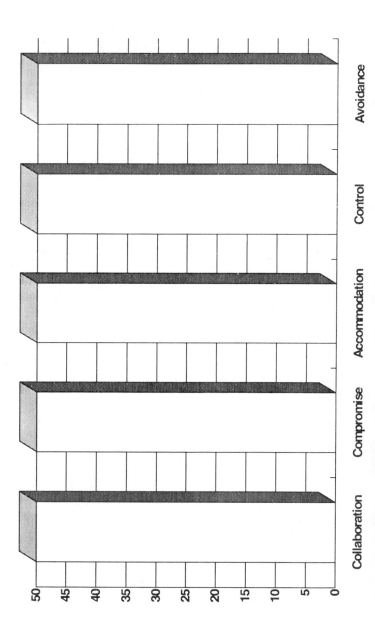

Determining Your Negotiating Style Profile

Transfer the total score for each style to the appropriate scale below:

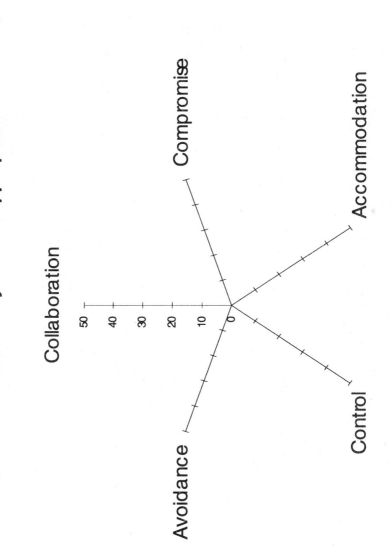

How to Prepare for the First Meeting

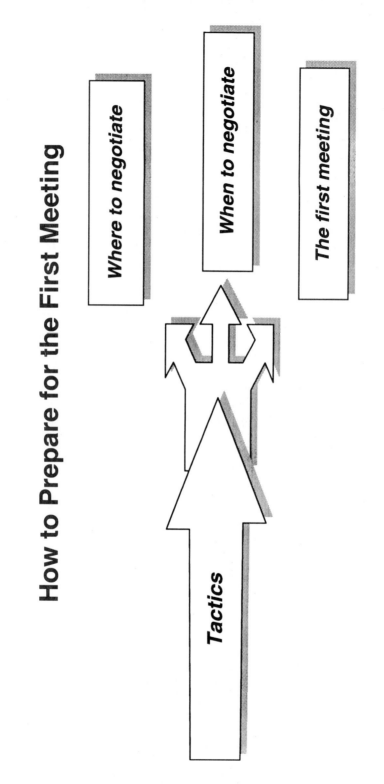

The Third Step of Negotiation

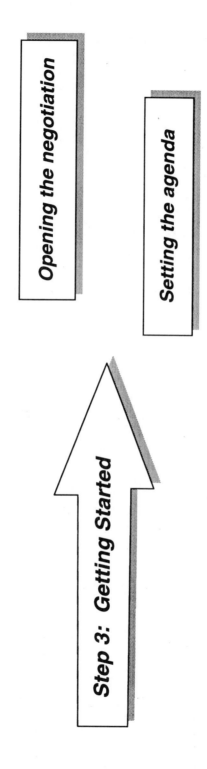

Step 3: Getting Started

Opening the negotiation

Setting the agenda

The Fourth Step of Negotiation

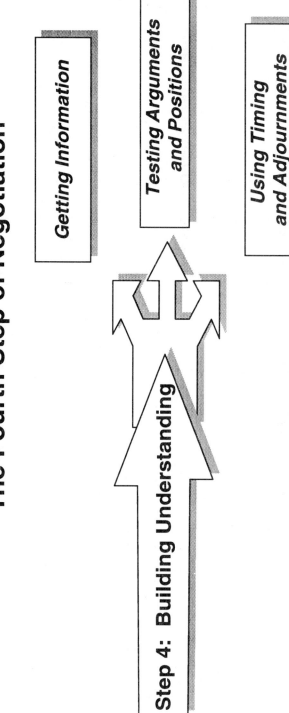

Getting Information

Testing Arguments
and Positions

Using Timing
and Adjournments

Step 4: Building Understanding

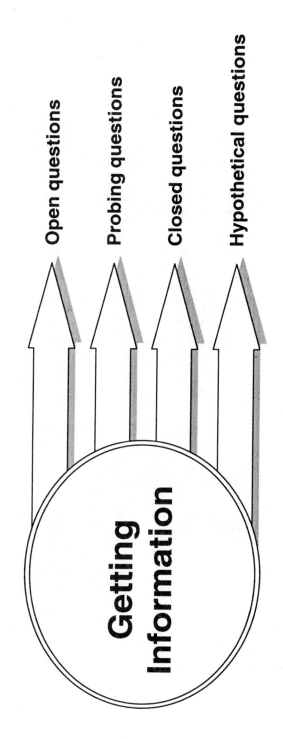

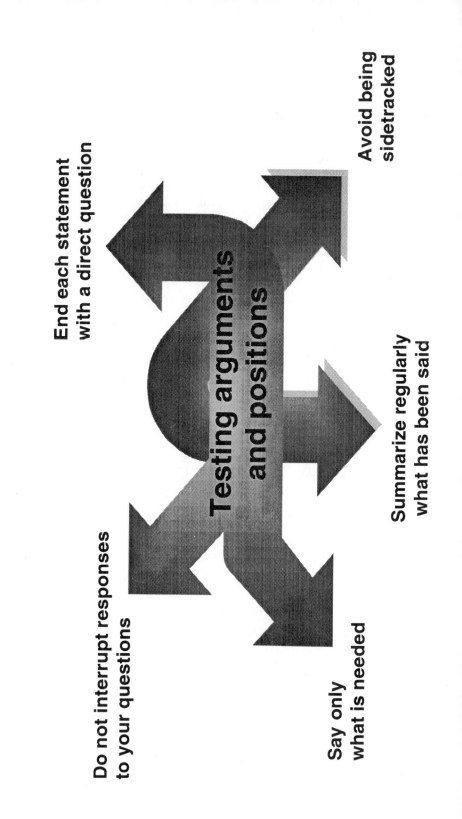

Testing arguments and positions

End each statement with a direct question

Avoid being sidetracked

Summarize regularly what has been said

Say only what is needed

Do not interrupt responses to your questions

The Fifth Step of Negotiation

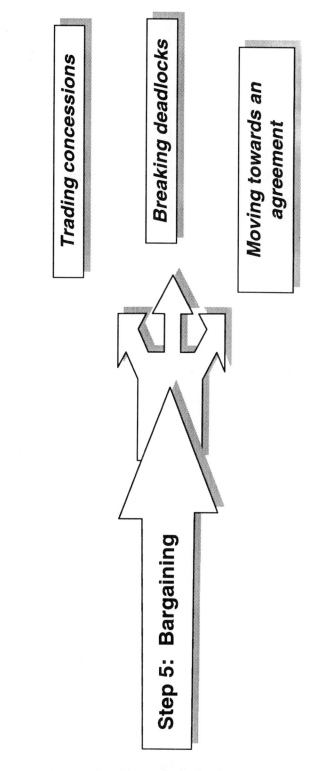

Trading concessions

Breaking deadlocks

Moving towards an agreement

Step 5: Bargaining

How to Trade Concessions

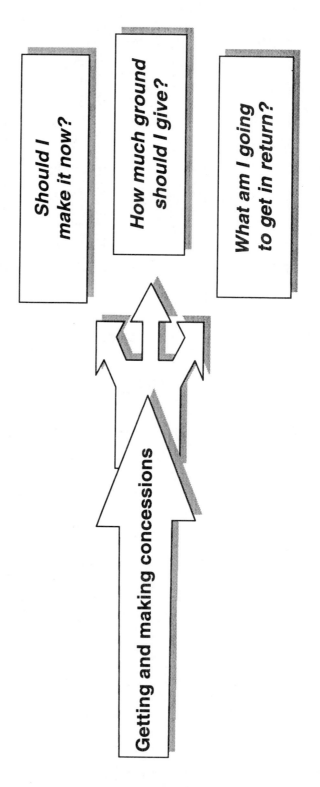

Should I
make it now?

How much ground
should I give?

What am I going
to get in return?

Getting and making concessions

Solving Problems within Groups

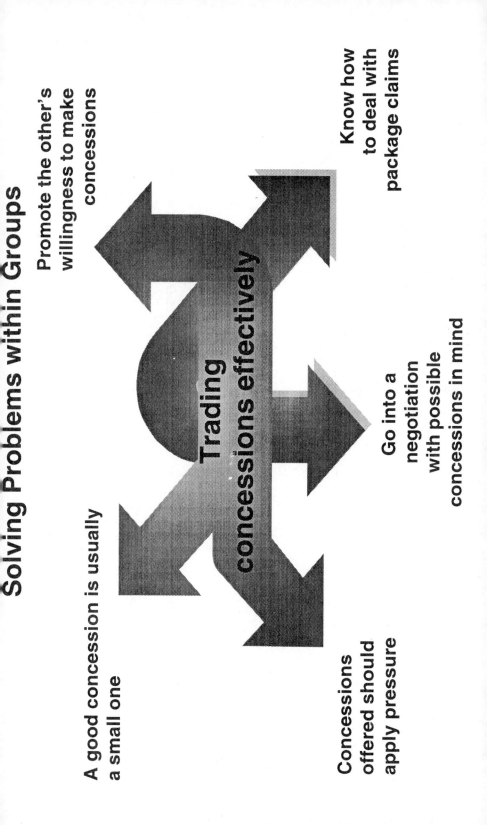

Trading concessions effectively

Promote the other's willingness to make concessions

Know how to deal with package claims

Go into a negotiation with possible concessions in mind

Concessions offered should apply pressure

A good concession is usually a small one

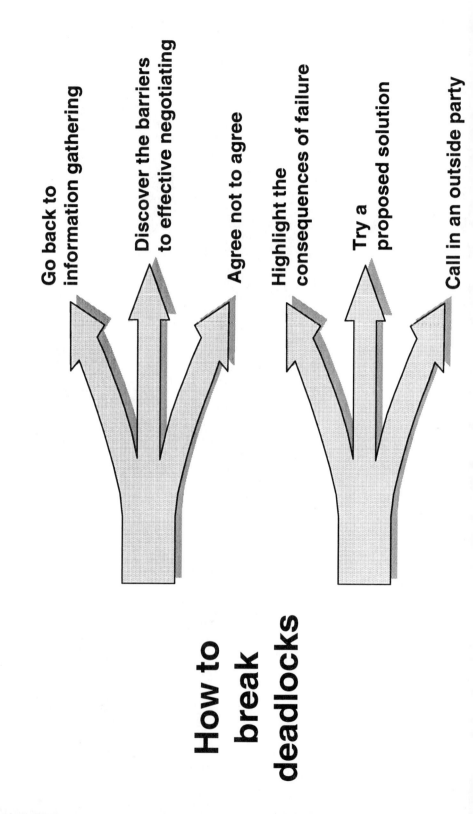

How to break deadlocks

Go back to information gathering

Discover the barriers to effective negotiating

Agree not to agree

Highlight the consequences of failure

Try a proposed solution

Call in an outside party

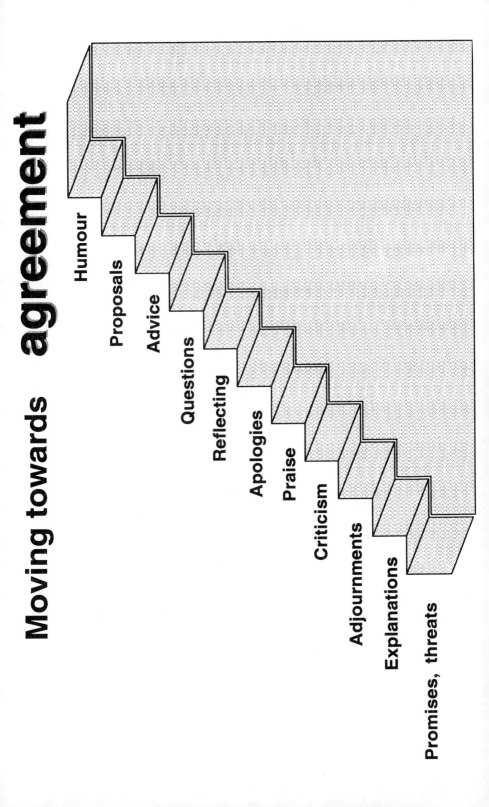

The Sixth Step of Negotiation

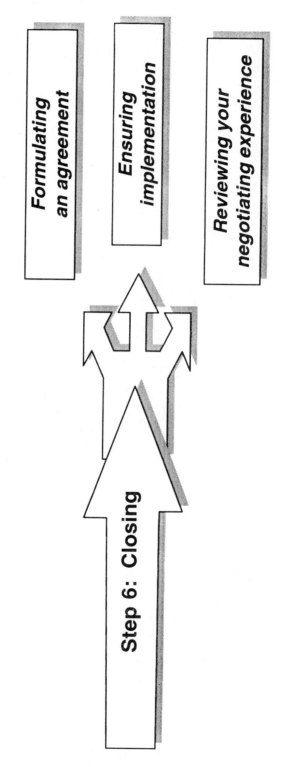

Step 6: Closing

Formulating an agreement

Ensuring implementation

Reviewing your negotiating experience

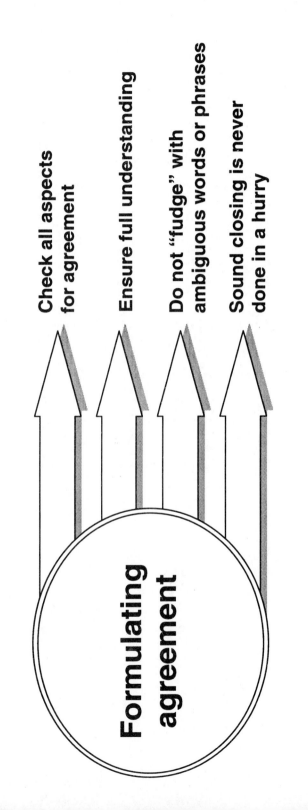

Formulating agreement

- Check all aspects for agreement
- Ensure full understanding
- Do not "fudge" with ambiguous words or phrases
- Sound closing is never done in a hurry

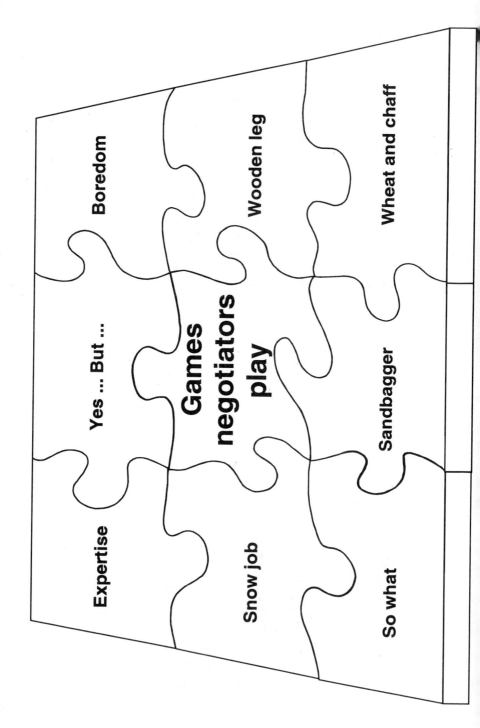

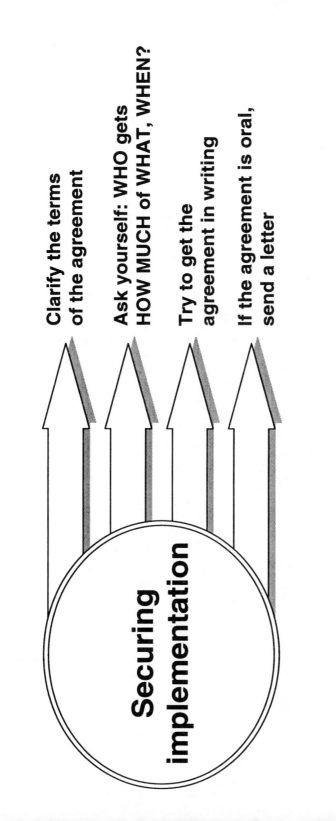

Securing implementation

- Clarify the terms of the agreement
- Ask yourself: WHO gets HOW MUCH of WHAT, WHEN?
- Try to get the agreement in writing
- If the agreement is oral, send a letter

Reviewing your negotiating experience

- How satisfied are you with the outcomes?
- Who was the most effective negotiator? Who conceded most?
- What strategies and actions helped most?
- What actions hindered the discussion?
- Did you trust the other party? What affected feelings most?
- How well was time used? Could it have been used better?
- How well did people listen to each other? Who talked most?
- Were creative solutions suggested? What happened to them?
- Did you understand well the other's underlying issues and concerns?
- How adequate was your preparation? How did this affect the negotiation?
- What were the strongest arguments put forth by the other party?
- How receptive was the other party to your arguments and ideas?
- What are your main learning points from this negotiation?
- What would you do differently next time?

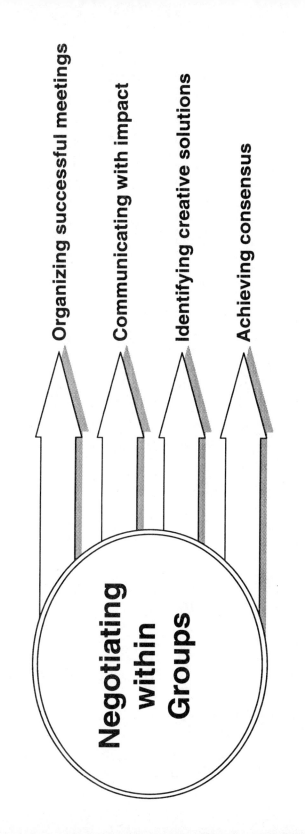

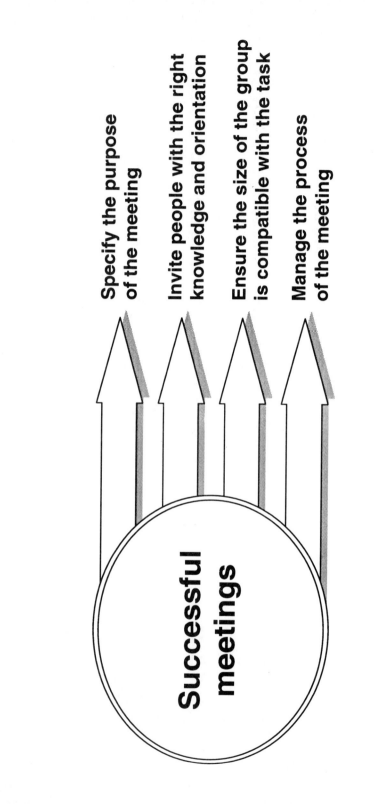

Specify the purpose
of the meeting

Invite people with the right
knowledge and orientation

Ensure the size of the group
is compatible with the task

Manage the process
of the meeting

Successful
meetings

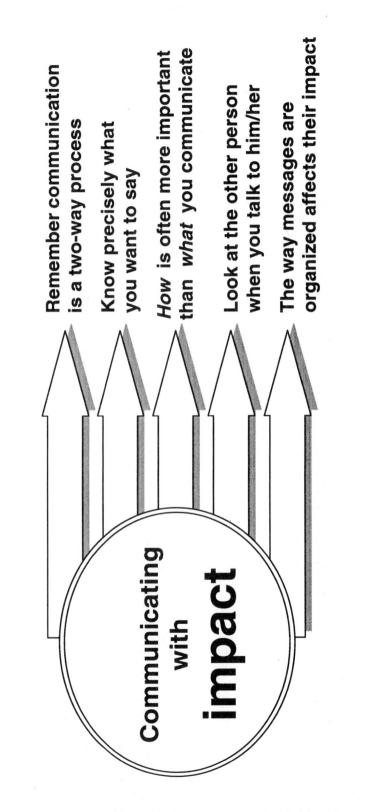

Solving Problems within Groups

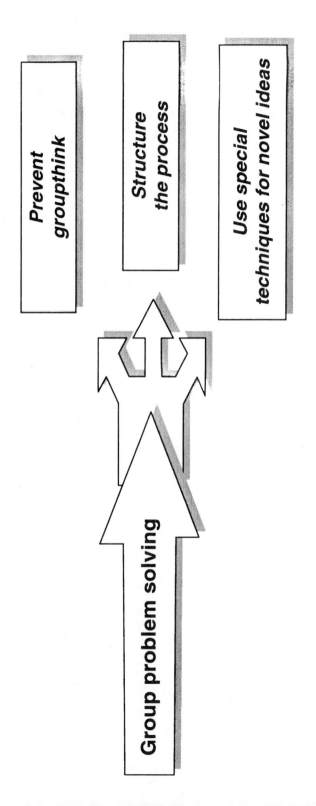

Group problem solving

Prevent groupthink

Structure the process

Use special techniques for novel ideas

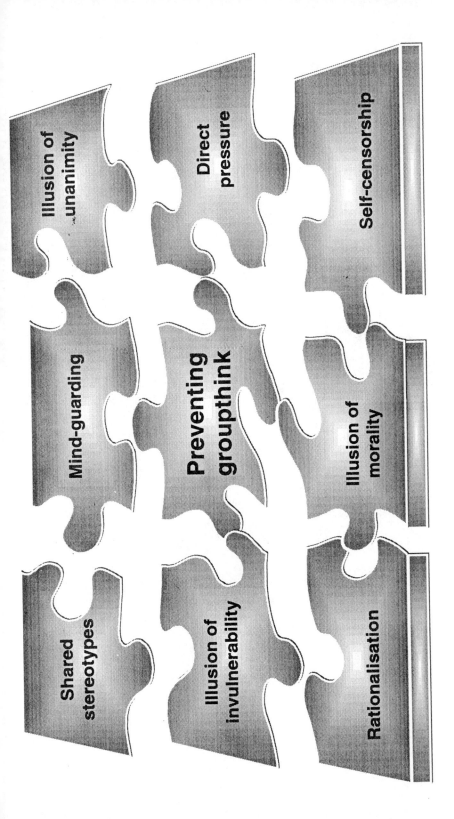

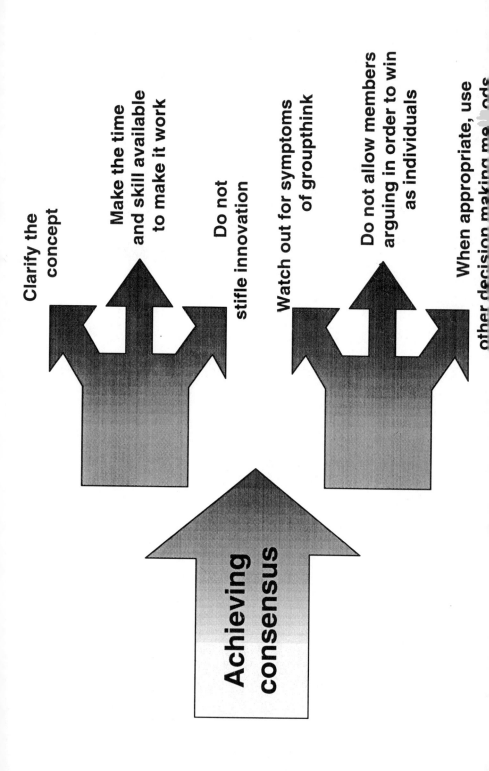

Achieving consensus

Clarify the concept

Make the time and skill available to make it work

Do not stifle innovation

Watch out for symptoms of groupthink

Do not allow members arguing in order to win as individuals

When appropriate, use other decision making methods

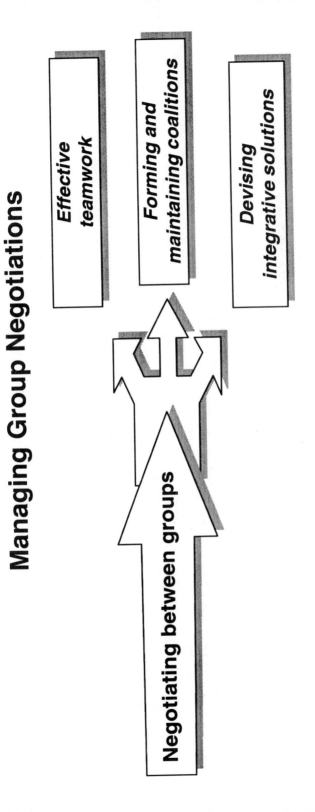

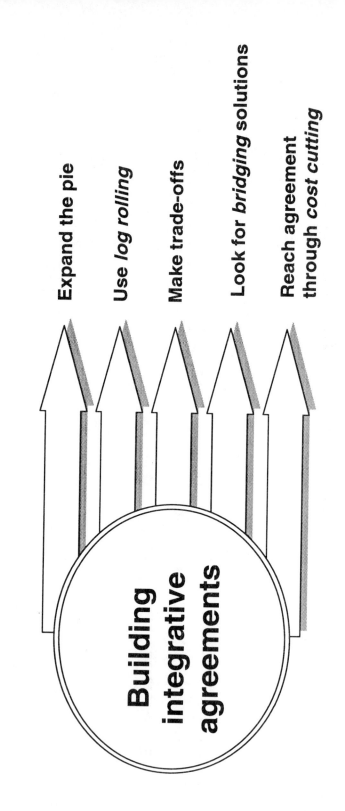

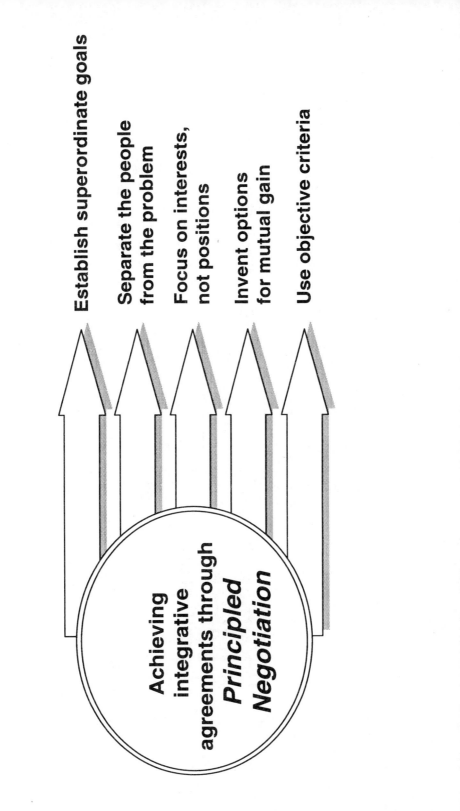

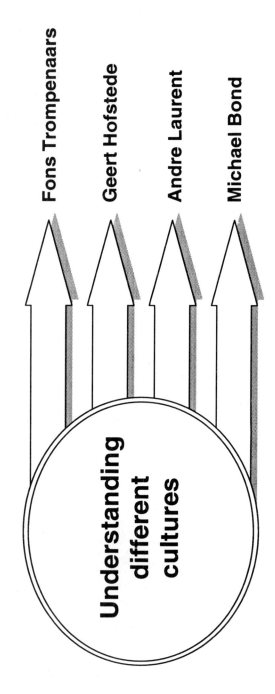

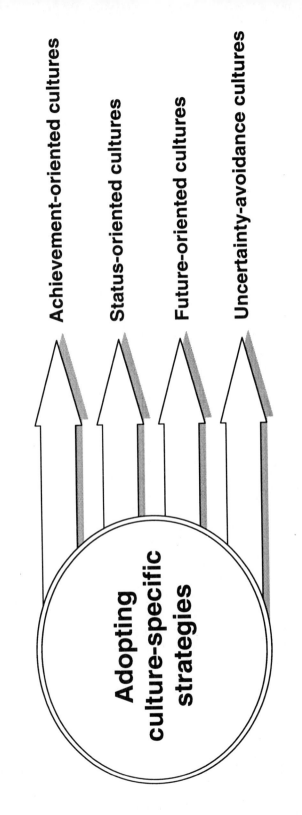

Index